PRAISE FOR *MY BEST FRIEND IS A WOOKIEE: A MEMOIR*

"I know I'm not the first person to ponder why Star Wars was such a touchstone in many people's lives. But I think what George Lucas did in creating a 'used universe' was make the fantastic and unimaginable accessible and relatable.

What Tony Pacitti has done with this book is kind of the same thing. In recounting his personal life journey and love affair with this not-always-loved film series, I believe he has found a commonality that we can all relate to. He has made the geeky accessible. For whom among us has not felt like an outsider at one time or another, or known the bliss and pain of falling in and out of love, or of going down paths in our life we knew we should not have?

This book will speak to many more people than Tony may realize because like Star Wars, it is an experience that has been shared by millions."

—Kevin Rubio, Writer/Director of *TROOPS*

"Tony Pacitti's *My Best Friend Is a Wookiee* is a hyperdrive tour through Star Wars fandom that's more fun than shooting womp rats in Beggar's Canyon. But it's also a comical, tender, no-punches-pulled coming-of-age memoir. We see a painfully shy kid slowly trying out the Jedi-like powers of adulthood and using the transformative Force (and forces) of the Star Wars universe to get him there. A heartbreaking work of staggering geekiness."

—Ethan Gilsdorf, Author of *Fantasy Freaks and Gaming Geeks: An Epic Quest for Reality Among Role Players, Online Gamers, and Other Dwellers of Imaginary Realms*

"Tony's journey starts in the safe haven of a childhood with the secret knowledge that *The Empire Strikes Back* is the greatest movie of all time, to a middle-school experience with the Special Editions, learning about midi-chlorians in high school, and finally reacting to the love of new, younger fans as an adult. Through bitter tears and explosive accomplishments, Tony reconnects us all with our youth in an intimate and powerful way. He uses hilarious language that's rich in nerd-minutiae with references firing off like Death Star quad-turbo-laser-cannons. But just like the drama of a favorite fantasy story settling into its place of ultimate importance in our own lives, this story is real and at times painful. When it's all said and done, we, the readers, find ourselves much like Chewbacca himself standing restrained next to the heartbroken who says, 'I love you' to a movie series. And, of course, the inevitable reply will come: 'I know.'"

—Scott Hinze, Host, Co-Creator of Fanboy Radio

"*My Best Friend Is a Wookiee* is the candid story of Tony's love affair with George Lucas's space opera. The movies were escape and consolation for a bullied, lonely kid in a new neighborhood; they helped him find companionship with other fans, inspired his creativity, and gave him something to cling to during the turbulence of puberty and junior high.

Tony's experiences aren't sugarcoated. He shows us that real-world 'rebels' are often deadbeat stoners; that sticking to your own beliefs can make you a loner; and that normal teenagers are neither pure-hearted heroes nor dark-side villains. Bullies can become friends, and nice guys can break hearts. But Tony's closing words carry a sense of generosity and the start of wisdom, and it's clear that Star Wars helped him get there."

—Will Brooker, Director of Research in Film and Television, Kingston University; Author of *Using the Force: Creativity, Community and Star Wars Fans*

MY BEST FRIEND IS A WOOKIEE

A MEMOIR

WITHDRAWN

MY BEST FRIEND IS A WOOKIEE

A MEMOIR

WITHDRAWN

ONE BOY'S JOURNEY
TO FIND HIS PLACE
IN THE GALAXY

TONY PACITTI

Avon, Massachusetts

Published by Adams Media,
a division of F+W Media, Inc.
57 Littlefield Street,
Avon, MA 02322. U.S.A.
www.adamsmedia.com

ISBN 10: 1-4405-0583-7
ISBN 13: 978-1-4405-0583-6
eISBN 10: 1-4405-0860-7
eISBN 13: 978-1-4405-0860-8

Printed in the United States of
America.

10 9 8 7 6 5 4 3 2 1

**Library of Congress Cataloging-in-
Publication Data**
Pacitti, Tony.
My best friend is a Wookiee : a
memoir / Tony Pacitti.
p. cm.
ISBN-13: 978-1-4405-0583-6
ISBN-10: 1-4405-0583-7
ISBN-13: 978-1-4405-0860-8
(eISBN)
ISBN-10: 1-4405-0860-7 (eISBN)
1. Pacitti, Tony—Childhood
and youth. 2. Star wars films—
Miscellanea. I. Title.
PN1995.9.S695P33 2010
791.43'75—dc22
[B]
2010019565

The excerpt on pages 199–200 is from
the article "It Will Be a Day Long
Remembered . . ." by Tony Pacitti.
Originally published on May 5, 2005
in Volume 51, Issue 27, of the UMass
Dartmouth *Torch*. Copyright © 2005
by UMass Dartmouth *Torch*. Used by
permission.

*This book is available at quantity
discounts for bulk purchases.
For information, please call
1-800-289-0963.*

To Mom and Dad.
This is all your fault. . . . I mean that in a good way.

Author's Note: The situations and characters in this book are all based off my memory of actual events. In some cases, names and traits have been changed and composite characters have been created. Otherwise this is my life, as I recall it, as a fanboy.

CONTENTS

EPISODE II

COOL AS TATOOINE

EPISODE III

LOVE AND LIGHTSABERS

PROLOGUE

In the summer of 2008 I was in the final stages of recovering from the Star Wars prequels. Over the years I had become one of those curmudgeonly, old fanboys who sat at his computer in his underpants raving like a madman whenever he heard news about a Star Wars spinoff or new DVD edition. I'd yell at these things the way your grandfather yells about how loud your music is or how much better life was before snowplows. For me, there had only ever been the three original Star Wars films, but for a while they seemed to be long gone. My memory of them was overshadowed by *Episode I, II,* and *III* and George Lucas's commitment to reimagining the movies I grew up with by way of digital wizardry.

Meanwhile, the films that had filled me with so much wonder, hope, and creative inspiration as a boy, the movies that had comforted me when I felt so afraid of trying to be the person I wanted to be, were still out there. But I had become so blinded by my disappointment that that special kind of cinematic lightning hadn't struck twice, I had been unable to see that.

Gradually I was able to make peace with my hatred of the prequels and move on. Old wounds were healing and the scars weren't nearly as bad as I had expected. So imagine my surprise when, seemingly out of the blue, a new Star Wars movie was set to drop out of hyperspace into a theater near me.

When *The Clone Wars* movie—which was in fact a pilot for the soon-to-air animated TV series—came out, my initial response was one of sheer horror and confusion. It was as if my dead best friend was suddenly reanimated and starving for brains, and was shuffling mindlessly down my driveway. I already had my worries about the upcoming show, but movies and television shows were apples and oranges. I was gearing up for *The Clone Wars* TV series with cautious curiosity, but buying tickets for the movie? That felt like someone was asking me to point out my would-be murderer in a lineup. I didn't know if I could stand Star Wars on the big screen again. At the same time, I began to suspect that facing the new movie could be empowering. If I faced up to it, I could tell it that what was done was done, that it couldn't hurt me anymore. It could do nothing to change how important the movies were to me. Either way, if I was going to face it, I needed some help.

One of my coworkers had a ten-year-old son named Marc. The boy was a full-fledged, all-out, balls-to-the-wall Star Wars nut. It was a fact he wore proudly on his sleeve: his mother had even brought him in to work one Halloween in a homemade Boba Fett costume. I was beyond impressed, and after a trip home to my parents' house, I returned with a stack of my old Star Wars novels, a gift from a once-bitter, old fanboy to a bright-eyed, young daydreamer. I saw a lot of my younger self in Marc. Just as I once had, Marc firmly believed that any Star Wars was good Star Wars.

I asked Marc's mother if the two of them would join me in what was sure to be ninety minutes of nonstop neon explosions, where the fun would be inversely proportional to the product placement. My mind was pretty much made up before I even saw the previews, but just below my jaded surface was a secret agenda: to be reminded how it felt to see Star Wars through the fresh eyes of a kid whose every waking thoughts were of Wookiees and lightsabers.

When I arrived at their house, Marc ran out the door to greet me in the driveway.

"I'm watching *Episode III*," he informed me, and then with a spooky voice and ten wiggly fingers, he intoned, "Reveeeenge of the Sith!"

I walked inside and plopped down on their couch, cringing through the banter between Yoda and the Emperor. Marc sat next to me, but he may as well have been billions of miles away, completely swept up in the action on the screen. He loved this movie as unequivocally as I loved *The Empire Strikes Back*.

"You know they used a puppet Yoda in the first one," he told me, referring to Yoda's scenes in *The Phantom Menace*.

"Oh yeah?" I replied, trying hard and failing miserably to swallow the bile rising in my throat and mirror his enthusiasm.

"They used computers for all the other ones."

There was a pause as he watched Yoda draw his lightsaber.

"Yeah," he continued, "computer Yoda is so much better."

The notion that a digitized Yoda could ever be better than Frank Oz with his hand up the business end of a Muppet was

exactly the kind of thing that got my Underoos all in a knot.
As far as Marc was concerned, the new trilogy trumped the old
one. Maybe I had misjudged the situation. What if instead of
helping me remember how great it was to be a kid experiencing Star Wars for the first time, I just ended up beating him up
and leaving him bleeding to death in a Dumpster somewhere?
I guess I could always plead the Forgotten Amendment, which
our forefathers included in the Secret Constitution, which
clearly states that any act of Star Wars–related aggression committed against a minor is automatically dismissed if the minor
willingly confesses to preferring CGI Yoda to Puppet Yoda.
(Don't look too closely into that legal argument.)

    We wolfed down a quick lunch before the movie, and I
picked Marc's brain about all things Star Wars. We talked
about Anakin's transformation from hero to Darth Vader, an
important narrative arc that I felt had been rushed but Marc
praised. After hearing his thoughts on Yoda I had expected this,
but he surprised me when we started talking about the paral-
lel love stories in each trilogy. He agreed that Han and Leia's
relationship was far more compelling than the one between
Anakin and Padmé.
    "That was sickening," he told me, though it was probably
because Anakin and Padmé's was a bit more mushy. Ten-year-
old boys don't do mushy.
    We discussed Star Wars' alien sidekicks Jar Jar and Chew-
bacca. Though Marc conceded that Chewie was the cooler
sidekick, he continued to defy all of my expectations with wild,
bogus claims like using a puppet for Yoda was cheesier than
anything Jar Jar Binks ever did, ever.

"Dude, you're kidding, right?" I asked—no, I begged.

"No way. I like him," he insisted. "He's blundering and innocent. He totally lightens the mood of intergalactic war."

Noticing the clock, I decided to wrap up the debate with something more specific—the Clone Wars. A major conflict that had been an integral part of the Star Wars mythology since the very first film, the Clone Wars themselves had been all but passed over in the last three installments. It was a struggle that fans had been dying to see since a hologram of Carrie Fisher had mentioned it in 1977. For Marc this made perfect sense. He thought that Anakin's personal character arc and his involvement in the Clone Wars would have gotten in the way of one another, so this, a film and then a companion animated series, seemed like the best way to show the war itself.

"Huh. You know what, Marc, I never thought of that."

"Yeah, no kidding!"

"Shuddup!"

As we walked into the theater, a very small, and very irritating, part of me started to panic. Looking around, I expected spikes to erupt from behind the posters and concession menus like an unused booby trap George Lucas had kicked around from the *Temple of Doom* days. When I approached the girl working the ticket booth, I waited for her to whisper, "Turn back! Turn back now before it's too late! Nothing but evil awaits you in auditorium six, third down on your left!" With paranoia starting to take hold, I nervously turned to Marc and asked him what he was expecting to get out of our impending ordeal.

"Comedy," he said. "Definitely some comedy. I mean, just look at the way it's animated!"

Marc wasn't too far off. The movie had a lot of what a kid his age would call great comedy. Things got silly right off the bat, when the bad guys kidnapped Jabba the Hutt's baby son. Then we met Anakin's new Padawan, Ahsoka, a smart-mouthed brat who seemed as if her personality was developed in focus-group hell. The two of them fight a lot of droids—who for whatever reason are all wise-cracking, sub-incompetent goofballs—save the baby Hutt, run around and generally get nothing done. The silliest part of the whole thing, however, was Jabba's uncle, Ziro the Hutt, who struck me as equal parts Oogie Boogie from *The Nightmare Before Christmas* and Nathan Lane's character from *The Birdcage*.

The movie jumped from one battle scene to another, and Marc's eyes flicked back and forth, soaking in every digitally rendered nanosecond of what he was clearly enjoying the ever-living crap out of. He leaned in for the quiet parts and waited patiently to be tossed back into his seat when an explosion rocked out of the sound system.

While Marc immersed himself completely in the experience, I was overassessing everything. *This isn't my Star Wars*, I thought. *No way in hell would I have bought into this when I was his age.*

We walked back to the car after the movie ended and I silently went over it again and again, feeling neither the hatred I had been expecting nor the pleasure I had been hoping for. Marc, on the other hand, hopped from one foot to another, all jacked up on having just done an hour-and-a-half-long line of eye-cocaine, and regaled us with a recap of what we had just watched as if we hadn't been there with him. He pantomimed lightsaber duels and recited his favorite droid one-liners. Then he looked up, a little out of breath, and a big toothy grin stretched wide across his round face.

"So. What did you think?" I asked.

"That. Was. Awesome." This wasn't an opinion, said his tone, but a fact. "*That* was a Star Wars movie."

Maybe he'll read this when he's my age and try to take those words back. Or maybe he won't. By all rights, the Ewoks are pretty lame, but I don't enjoy *Return of the Jedi* any less. They get a pass on my grown-up sensibilities because of my childhood attachment to them. I always sort of knew this, but it wasn't until I sat down with Marc, who spoke to me on behalf of a generation who had been raised on this new brand of Star Wars, that I was really willing to admit that.

Watching and talking about Star Wars with Marc didn't do exactly what I had hoped it would. I didn't suddenly find myself in love with the new movies, but I found something when I saw his face erupt with pure, unbridled joy because of what was happening on the screen in front of us. In his eyes I saw a spark, a glimmer of something that this big, weird, wonderful world of make-believe stirred inside him. It's the same spark you would have seen in my eyes sixteen years earlier, back in the summer of '92, when I had my first look at a galaxy far, far away. . . .

EPISODE I

A FANBOY IS BORN

CHAPTER 1

SAGA GENESIS

IT WAS THE PERFECT DAY to get socked in the face with clumps of wet dirt. The ambush ended as quickly as it started, a flashflood of dirty projectiles and savage war cries from my hidden assailants. Slowly, with my head down and my tail between my legs, I walked home, picking clumps of mud out of my hair and wiping tears from my cheeks. What little self-esteem I'd had was shattered on the corner of my street like shards of a broken mirror, reflecting the laughing, loose-tooth faces of the jerks who had pelted me with filth. I was seven years old, living in a new house in a new town, and had just been introduced to the rest of the guys in my neighborhood by way of elementary-school guerilla tactics. The friends I had were a half-hour car ride away. Given our inability to see each other and the fickle minds of seven-year-olds, they felt as tangible as imaginary friends.

I have always worn my emotions on my sleeve, and that day was no exception. I may as well have been wearing a T-shirt with a picture of me getting kicked in the nuts while simultaneously getting a wedgie, having my lunch money stolen, and having my heart ripped out through my mouth. Mom knew that no "Things will get better" talk, no matter how inspirational the accompanying music, was going to fix what had happened that afternoon. Her boy needed some real cheering up.

In the bathroom, while she helped clean the crud off my face with a towel fresh out of the dryer, she looked at me with eyes that always seemed to smile and asked the question: "Have you seen *Star Wars* yet?"

My love affair with the galaxy far, far away was to begin with the second Star Wars movie, *The Empire Strikes Back*. Mom dug a videotape out of a box jammed full of tapes with movies and cartoons that had been recorded from TV. According to the peeling, orange Kodak label on the spine of the tape, this one was a sci-fi double feature my Dad had bootlegged from HBO, with *Empire* playing second to David Lynch's *Dune*. As Mom fast-forwarded to the spot where she thought *Empire* should start, she cracked open the ironing board, looking to kill a couple of birds with one stone while she watched the movie with me.

The tape was snowy and the sound a bit warbled at the tail end of *Dune*'s credits, where it segued less than gracefully into the HBO logo from the late 1980s.

"The following film is rated PG," the tape declared in a generic male American voice. The rating didn't mean anything to me, but as the required bits of boilerplate legalese—rating, content, closed captioning—were rattled off, I became very eager about what I was about to see. I knew Star Wars by reputation only and couldn't tell you a thing about it at the time. All

I knew was that in a moment I was going to experience something monumental. Something very important. It was just a feeling I had, something deep in my gut.

When that epic Twentieth Century Fox drumroll began, it snapped me to attention. The machine-gun drumming of sticks and mallets hammered away the shame I was feeling about that afternoon's ambush and demanded that I turn myself over completely to what was about to play out on the television. One screen faded to another, from the Fox logo to a black title card with Slimer green letters that read "Lucasfilm, Ltd." The screen faded again, taking the sound with it, and for the first time in my life I was conscious of seeing the words "A long time ago in a galaxy far, far away...." It was a moment that felt like several lifetimes.

I hung on that moment, soaking in the image of those words and permanently burning them into my retinas. When I blink, those blue letters still flash against the darkness on the back of my eyelids. When the lights go out, those words are plastered over the void. They chilled me down to the marrow and had me leaning off the couch cushion, begging for more after getting so little. Those few words were perfect in my seven-year-old eyes. They promised so much. Hinted at amazing feats. Such good. Such evil. With so little, an entire galaxy was opened up for me to explore. Star Wars had me at "hello."

Suddenly that brief yet seemingly infinite silence was devastated by a blazing sonic assault. The opening fanfare from the London Symphony Orchestra hit me square in the face, shoving me hard into my seat. If seeing the words "A long time ago in a galaxy far, far away ..." was a first kiss, then hearing that first chord of the Star Wars theme was my cherry getting popped. Scratch that—this was bigger, more important than a sex metaphor could ever possibly illustrate. My life was beginning again that day. It was a rebirth.

As the trumpets roared across space and the words "Star Wars" rocketed into view, I felt like I was exploding out of the womb and into a world that I had always sensed around me as I'd gestated for seven years. The title, *The Empire Strikes Back*, soared up into view, followed by a text scroll that alluded to things that were intimidating and foreign yet strangely familiar. Death Star. Freedom fighters. Luke Skywalker. Darth Vader. These words stood out to me like masked doctors looking down at my squirming, goo-coated newborn body. Darth Vader was the only name that rang any sort of bell. When I read it, an image flashed into my head of a toothbrush my aunt had given me with an evil-looking, black-clad space man on it. It was a toothbrush I had once kept at my grandparents' house. "Dark Radar," I had called him, the words Darth and Vader having no meaning at that time in my young lexicon. Maybe that toothbrush had been a sign, a marker on a road that was meant to lead me to this point. I would go into the bathroom just to take that toothbrush out of its holder and look at him. Vader's evil image, looming like death itself, stared back at me through those darkened helmet lenses.

"Brush your teeth or else!" Or else what?

For two hours I sat fixated on the TV. My parents were Trekkies, so I had grown up watching a new episode of *Star Trek: The Next Generation* every Sunday and syndicated reruns most afternoons. Sci-fi techno-babble was plentiful, but the action was limited. No matter what the stakes were, no matter how perfect the Romulan or Borg plot seemed to be, the crew of the *Enterprise* always came out on top, thanks to Hollywood science and some good ol' moral fiber.

Empire was something else altogether. This was a world where science and magic came head to head. There were no illusions of peace or any safe havens aboard glamorous starships. There were no glamorous starships. X-Wings and the *Millennium Falcon* were the sci-fi versions of old hot rods and beat-around trucks. In this place, hope and annihilation were spoken within the same breath. Trust couldn't be taken for granted. Nothing was a sure thing. Heroes were always on the run, scraping by on anything they could get their hands on, while the bad guys had limitless resources to find them and smoke them out. This, kids, was a whole new ballgame.

Before he could even do anything in the movie, this Luke guy, whom I was meeting for the first time, was mauled by some nasty-looking space yeti. I couldn't have been more scared. This was the Luke the text scroll was talking about, and he was down for the count just two minutes in! Then Han told everyone he was leaving, and Leia started yelling at him. So far all the good guys were either unconscious or pissed off at each other. This was the antithesis of anything I had ever seen on *Star Trek* and went against what I had come to understand as basic movie logic. There was conflict, real human struggle, going on here. And robots! And that big hairy guy who looked like a real alien and not just a guy with latex skull-ridges slapped onto his forehead and some prop snaggleteeth in his mouth.

Starting with the second in a three-movie series, I felt overwhelmed by a history I knew nothing about. The characters' relationships were already established, the villains' motives were unclear, and I was bombarded with images I struggled to understand. When the Rebel snowspeeders were systematically blown out of the sky by the Empire's awesome, mechanical quadrupeds, I panicked. *Why*, I asked myself, *are the good guys losing so soon?* I looked over to my mom for a sign, some sort of indication as to why this was happening. She was locked onto the action on the screen, her focus daring me to keep watching. Her ironing never faltered.

Things didn't let up. This was just the first act, and as the movie moved on from the Battle of Hoth, the momentum built and the stakes kept rising. As the *Millennium Falcon* ducked and weaved its way through asteroids, narrowly avoiding certain destruction at the hands of space rocks, with the Empire in hot pursuit, I gnawed my nails to the bone. Nothing, and I mean nothing, was cooler than seeing that hunk of junk outclass those TIE fighters, luring them face first into asteroid after asteroid, or Han deducing that they were parked in the belly of a giant space slug. I sat there in my living room, watching this tiny ship fly up out of a crater, only to have this giant thing pop out and try to snap its jaws down on it. It was clearly a case of, "Well, our heroes dodged that bullet, how can we shake things up and put them back into the Empire's crosshairs? A space slug, that's how!" And it worked! It was just one item on a newly formed, rapidly growing grocery list of the coolest things I'd ever seen.

Yoda brought with him a much-needed sense of levity to the harrowing spectacle that had preceded Luke's arrival on Dagobah. The film so far had been a montage of pushing the good guys down and kicking them while they were there. A little green man with a funny voice and a Dennis the Menace sort of knack for irritating people was a nice break. *Man, I thought, I bet Yoda's gonna be like a kung fu master and this is totally the goofy, comic relief sidekick.* Wrong. They were one and the same, and like Luke, I bought into Yoda's cover—hook, line, and sinker. When Yoda switched from goofball to guru, I couldn't believe it. Everything that movie threw at me was a curveball, and I kept swinging. The challenge to get a hit was addictive, but I'd never connect with a pitch. Even a sure thing like Han's friend Lando proved to be just one of countless twists in the exhausting, curving road of *The Empire Strikes Back*.

But none of the twists compared to the climax of Luke and Vader's epic confrontation. Lightsabers clashed with that classic electric nails-on-a-chalkboard screech. Vader fought dirty, using his mastery of the Force to throw anything in his sight at Luke, knocking him off his guard, off his feet, and through plate glass. Here was a villain who threw the rule book out the window. He was evil incarnate, and nothing would stop him from completing his wicked crusade. Though Luke seemed outmatched, he never gave up. Maybe this was it. Maybe after all of that struggling the movie would remember that good will always triumph over evil. I knew that that's what would happen. Then Luke's hand got hacked off, and we both made the painful discovery that Darth Vader, yes Dark Radar himself, was his father. I wanted to scream. I wanted to cry out just like Luke did.

After a relentless two hours, the heroes, minus Han, managed to escape with their tails between their legs. For the first time since the movie had started, I took pause to think about my own defeat earlier that afternoon. Like the Rebels, I'd found myself outnumbered by a larger group of jerks who seemed to have all the resources necessary to make my life a hell for no particular reason. I didn't ask them to throw dirt at me. I didn't even know who they were. They were a faceless enemy. They didn't even have the decency to send their Darth Vader out to intimidate me first.

As the movie ended, I felt drained. Watching Luke and Leia stare out the medical ship's window as the *Falcon* flew away, with that sad music playing as the defeated Rebel fleet floated solemnly through space, was almost too much to handle. Nothing good happened to the people it normally happened to. Nothing. It was the first instance I could recall of a movie ending on such a real, sour note, and I absolutely loved it.

Without knowing it, I had become a participant in the lives of these characters, a soldier for the Rebel Alliance. They were as real to me as they were fantasy. Han was a bastard—sarcastic, cocky, shortsighted—but there was a hero under all those scoundrelly layers. He was flawed, which was something I had never noticed or wanted from my movie heroes before. Leia was as far from a damsel in distress as she could possibly be, but ultimately—and despite her best efforts to the contrary—she fell victim to her own love for a pirate. Luke Skywalker, true-blue hero of the day that he was, was in the middle of a crisis of faith. These three characters were faced with the most daunting challenges of their lives, and many of those challenges came from within. I came for the lasers and the spaceships, but I stayed for the deep, personal struggle that these characters were dealing with. But don't get me wrong, the lasers and spaceships have always been a plus.

What really hit the movie home for me was that, despite all they'd gone through, they still clung to hope. Though one of them was gone, he could still be saved if his friends played their cards right. The rest of them, bloodied, bruised, and scared, lived to fight another day. That meant something to me. I know now that they would come out on top in the next one, but at the time their futures felt completely up in the air. In all the movies I had ever seen, the hero would hit that point somewhere in the middle of the film, when there was still time for him to save the day. But in *Empire* there was no time left. The three of us—Luke, Leia, and I—had to wait for the sequel to take up arms one more time against the forces of evil. But they had not given up; you see it when they look out into space. You hear it in Lando's voice when he leaves with Chewbacca to track down Han. They all have hope.

So there I was, a seven-year-old boy in a new house in a new town, being terrorized by the older kids in the neighborhood and fearing to death the mere thought of a new school. I didn't know any of the rules that any of the people in this strange new place lived by. I had no Obi-Wan or Yoda to lead me through it. I was flying blind, having a crisis of faith in myself that would last for the next decade and change. All I had was this new house to hide in and this new movie full of wonderful things to keep me company. To give me hope.

I don't know how many times I watched that worn-out tape over the course of the next few months, but it never got much of a rest. At one point, I thought I could smell the film sizzling in the plastic shell. I wished I had a giant Wookiee for a best friend to keep the bullies at bay. I'd go to the grocery store with my mom and wave my hand in front of the automatic doors, opening them hands-free like a real Jedi. Driving with my dad, I'd pretend that the cars in front of us on 95 North were asteroids, the ones behind us were TIE fighters, and that his beat-up, funky-smelling '87 Ford Ranger was a beat-up, funky-smelling YT-1300 light freighter called the *Millennium Falcon*. John Williams's music filled my head throughout the day, and if you asked me at any point between that fateful day and the end of the sixth grade, I'd tell you that the person I most wanted to be when I grew up was the man who had just given me this glorious gift of wonder and adventure: George Lucas.

CHAPTER 2

LIFE BEFORE STAR WARS

THERE IS A LEGEND IN our family that says my folks took me to see a triple-header of the Star Wars trilogy at a drive-in. I was six months old at the time, so it wasn't really a formal introduction for me as much as it was a revisiting for my parents. At that point, the summer of '85, *Return of the Jedi* was just over two years old, and there I was, six months out of the womb and only capable of processing things like hunger, pain, and joy on the most basic levels and only operating in two modes: screaming and not screaming. For a while I thought that maybe this family story was just some urban myth thought up to explain the one obsession I've ever really had. But Mom and Dad confirmed it. I sat there in a sweaty little Toyota while my parents sat back, watched, and—gross—probably made out during Star Wars.

It would seem that fate brought me together with Luke, Han, and Leia on that hot summer's eve in the dawn of my life.

Like a lump of Play-Doh, and probably just as squishy, I was ripe for the molding. It is quite possible that as that night went on, as the lasers fired, the lightsabers blazed, and the Force surrounded us, my DNA was rewritten, replacing the occasional A, G, and T with a 3, P, and O. It was there. It has always been there, a part of me, even before I knew it. I was like Luke in *A New Hope*—his destiny as the greatest Jedi of all time was written even when he hadn't ever heard of the Force. My destiny lay with these movies.

By the time I became so intimately acquainted with the movies, they had long been established as a pop-culture juggernaut. Star Wars immediately became something bigger than just a movie. It was the Force itself, surrounding and penetrating all aspects of life. I really had no choice about being sucked into the world of high adventure and sci-fi mysticism that they created. The films are so engrained into our intrinsic cultural awareness that you don't need to have seen them to get jokes and references to them. Take my earliest memory of Star Wars in my pre–Star Wars years: an episode of *Muppet Babies*.

In the episode, Nanny gave the kids a video camera to play with. To fit the whole gang into a movie, they decided to make their own version of a film with a lot of characters, so they picked *Star Wars*. Complete with clips from the actual movie, the gang dressed up as Kermit Skyhopper, Fozziebacca, and Princess Piggy.

It was cute. It was faithful to the movie in that kids-show kind of way, and it was enough to plant the seeds of familiarity in me for certain *Star Wars*–related images. I suddenly had in my mind's Rolodex a frame of reference for TIE fighters, lightsabers, and the Death Star. They were all just as alien and exotic as you'd expect artifacts from another galaxy to be, and they projected a sense of wonder and cool that struck a deeper chord with me than anything else I had encountered in the scant few years of my life.

Muppet Babies may have been the first of many flirtations during the early days of my courtship with Star Wars, but of all of the dominoes that were set into place during my life of rabid fandom, one of my fondest was the Star Tours ride at Disney World.

Our parents swept us—an excited five-year-old me and my three-year-old sister, Amanda, who probably wouldn't be able to appreciate the wonders of Disney World on the mature level that I did—away for a week of make-believe and good old-fashioned price gouging. As far as Dad was concerned, the whole trip's success or failure rested on his getting a giant turkey leg from a snack shack on Frontier Land. He could take or leave the rides, though he leaned toward the leave side for anything that went too fast or got you too wet.

Amanda quickly developed an unhealthy obsession with the "It's a Small World" ride. As the bubbling cauldrons of testosterone that we were, my Dad and I decided that five times in a row was our limit and had Mom drag her screaming behind us to something much more macho, like the Dumbo ride or a fried dough stand.

A few days into the trip we were at MGM Studios and I caught my first glimpse of a giant, four-legged machine standing guard over one of the attractions. This hulking, mechanical beast and the movie ride residing beneath it all seemed to resonate with a faint echo of a memory, like Luke's feelings of familiarity on Dagobah. I was about to get as close to stepping into the world of Star Wars as possible without some awesome, drug-fueled hallucination.

The ride was alive in the sort of way that only Disney and a child's imagination can pull off. Nothing looked cheap or phony and every sound seemed to emanate from an actual spaceship or droid. Making our way through the line, my family and I found ourselves in a functioning interstellar travel terminal. Advertisements for exciting voyages to strange, faraway planets beckoned us while an animatronic C-3PO and R2-D2 bickered in areas off limits to vacationers.

My excitement made waiting to get on the actual ride bearable, as opposed to waiting in line for an underwhelming spin in a pastel teacup. When we finally got to the end of the line and strapped into our seats aboard the StarSpeeder 3000, we were whipped through a whirlwind tour of the galaxy far, far away. Our tour guide, a spastic little droid, should have had his license revoked. We narrowly dodged comets, overshot our destination, and wound up smack in the middle of a battle between the Rebels and the Empire. With each asteroid collision, laser blast, and Death Star explosion, our seats rocked and shook. For the few minutes my family and I sat in that can-shaped room, with its shocks, hydraulics, and speakers all locked in perfect synchronization with the video display, we were no longer bound to our boring blue planet. I forgot that we were in a place built on the foundation of making dreams reality, and when we left the ride I didn't look back on what I had just experienced as just another roller coaster. I had gone to space, battled with an evil empire, and come back to tell the tale.

A couple of days later I caught a glimpse of the trash-compactor scene from *A New Hope* in our hotel room. Had it not been for the fact that we were at the happiest damn place on Earth, I probably would have sat there and watched the rest of the movie. Instead we just barely crossed paths, like two starships passing in the night.

Over all too quickly, our trip to Disney ended and we returned to my early childhood home in Lynn, Massachusetts: "Lynn, Lynn, the city of sin," as the town's unofficial slogan went. Obi-Wan calls Mos Eisley "a wretched hive of scum and villainy." Lynn wasn't Mos Eisley by any stretch of the imagination, and regardless of whatever a goofy rhyme implied might have been lurking just outside our neighborhood, our parents all felt safe enough to let us roam around, though none of us kids ever went more than a few houses away in any given direction.

If I wasn't in my own backyard, I was in one of three others: BJ's, Jen's, or Ben's. BJ was the kind of kid who would push you on a swing so you could both brag about being there when you swung the highest of anyone on the block. Meanwhile he'd be waiting behind you with a wiffle-ball bat, poised like a big-league slugger, ready to crack the back of your skull out of the park. I never saw it coming, but Mom managed to intercept him before he dealt the killing blow.

Ben was an older boy whose word, to us pups at least, was gospel. Any outrageous claims he made, like the one about how the star-shaped Popsicles at Dairy Queen were so sharp that they'd slice your tongue and gums wide open, became instant fact. We believed him because he was bigger—and therefore smarter—and he knew how to get all the warp whistles in Super Mario Bros. 3. He clearly had the credentials to be taken seriously all the time.

And then there was Jen, the lone girl in the pack. I knew her before boys and girls thought the opposite sex was icky and before words like nerd and loser became my professional titles. Jen and I were best friends, a pact we sealed with a kiss behind the Little Tykes playhouse in her backyard. We were two little kids whose secret world existed in the short bursts of time between right before breakfast and not long after dinner. There was no yesterday and no tomorrow, just a never-ending string of afternoons. The only thing that ever changed was the weather. We lived with the constants of being best friends, and as far as we knew, that would never change.

Even more vividly than I can remember playing with other kids in my Lynn neighborhood, I remember playing alone. Dad had finished the attic of our house, transforming a large part of it into a playroom for me and Amanda and a smaller corner into an office for himself, where he'd labor over blueprints, bids, and budgets for the construction company where he worked. I would spend hours up there building trucks and castles out of DUPLO blocks or saving the streets with my Ninja Turtles action figures. And I loved TV. Loved it. Yet as much as I loved the *Teenage Mutant Ninja Turtles*, *Thundercats*, and any other crime-fighting humanoid/animal supergroup, there was an extra-special place in my heart for the two inter-dimensional portals we had plugged into the back of our big, late '70s model, 19-inch Magnavox: the VCR and the Nintendo.

E.T. and *Back to the Future* were both in heavy rotation, probably more than any other movies we had in the house. I spent so much time with them that they may as well have been my surrogate parents. When Mom and Dad weren't dol-ing out life lessons, I was learning all I needed to from those two movies. *E.T.* was a pile of dry leaves that Star Wars ignited into the wildfire of my youthful imagination. While other kids cowered at the sight of Elliot's very own alien, I sat mesmerized, wishing that someday a friend from another world would follow a trail of Reese's Pieces into my house.

E.T.'s influence on me could be seen at a very early age, such as the time I took a page from Elliot's book and called my grandmother "Penis Breath." I couldn't have been anymore than four the day my grandparents came over to visit and I decided to greet them with one of the movie's lesser-known lines.

"Hello, sweetheart," Gram said, a nice big smile on her kind old face.

"It's nothing like that, Penis Breath!" I replied, not entirely sure why my grandmother was suddenly beset with a simultaneous stroke and heart attack, as indicated by her bulging, cartoon eyes and a shrill, glass-shattering wail of terror. It turns out my grandmother was less offended by the notion that I had accused her of eating loads of dick than she was by my usage of the proper terminology for said member. Gram belonged to the school of thought that believed little kids should only know little-kid words for such a horrible, horrible organ. If I'd called her "Doodle Breath," the whole scenario would have been received with a laugh. Instead, *E.T.* was temporarily pulled from rotation after its next viewing, when my Mom discovered the source of my filthy mouth.

Back to the Future, with its own fair share of potty talk, was played almost as often as *E.T.* I'd sit up close to the TV screen and yell lines like "What the hell's a gigawatt?!" and "Great Scott!" while mowing down bowls of mac and cheese. In the same way that I wanted an alien for a best friend, I wanted to know a mad scientist. I imagined the three of us would have gotten along great, traveling through time as Doc Brown and I enriched our otherworldly friend's understanding of human history. Plus Marty played a mean guitar, an enviable trait if ever there was one. I saw *BTTF* more times than *E.T.* growing up just because of the ridiculous amount of TV airtime it got. No matter how far into the movie, if we came across it while channel-surfing, my family felt obligated to sit there and watch the rest of it.

Much like *Muppet Babies, E.T.* and *Back to the Future* both had a handful of Star Wars reference. While dressed in a radiation suit and armed with a blow dryer, Marty McFly tells his father that he is an extra-terrestrial named Darth Vader. Elliot shares his collection of Star Wars figures with E.T. in one of the movie's earlier heartfelt moments, and later, while out trick or treating, E.T. points to a kid dressed as Yoda and moans "Hoooome!" These were funnier after actually seeing *Star Wars*, but at the time they still got a little chuckle out of me, even if they did go totally over my head.

And then there was Nintendo, that beautiful, little gray box. I remember unwrapping it one Christmas and having no idea what it was. Based on the packaging alone, which showed the console and the bright red Zapper against a glowing, star-filled sky, I knew that it was going to be one of the coolest things ever. While movies showed me strange, faraway lands, my Nintendo let me run around in them, eat a few mushrooms, and bust some Koopa skulls. Even twenty years later video games can't come up in conversation without my folks laughing at how I'd sit with controller in hand, tongue out like Michael Jordan, and bounce around in my seat as if it would help Mario get over a ditch, or how I'd play *Duck Hunt* with the muzzle of the Zapper pressed up against the TV screen.

With my life's hobbies picked by the time I was six, I was fully prepared to commit myself to a life on the couch, till death do us part. The thought of ever having to leave my TV seemed stupid to me. Why go outside and play with a goober like BJ when I could play with Mario and Luigi? Taking care of my sister took up a chunk of my parents' time, and I was content in front of the TV. In an effort to get me out a bit more, Mom and Dad signed me up for soccer. Even at that early age, when all a little kid should want to be doing is running around chasing a ball, my interests lay elsewhere. Halfway through my first soccer game I heard someone shooting off fireworks, so I stopped running to tell my mom about it.

"Ma!" I yelled. "Ma! Listen! Firecrackers!"

I guarantee that Mom thought that it was the funniest thing she had ever seen, with me standing there in the middle of the field yelling toward the stands while the game continued around me. Dad must have been mortified. My father was, and still is, very much a Guy with a capital *G*, and he has every *Sports Illustrated* swimsuit issue since 1976 to prove it. Give the man a six-pack of beer, a ball game, and the *Three Stooges*, and he'll be all set for the day.

But as much of a Guy as Dad is, he's also a pretty big nerd, despite how much he refuses to accept it. This is the man who raised me on *Star Trek: The Next Generation*, who re-reads the Dune and Lord of the Rings books every few years. If the Red Sox aren't playing, you can find him sitting with a gin and tonic in front of the TV on a Friday night to watch three hours of Syfy. His favorite superhero is the Mighty Thor—and no one but a nerd would claim Thor as his favorite. When I was nine he holed himself up in the bathroom with my *Death of Super-man* comic before I even got a chance to crack the spine. The man was willing to put a Borg Institute of Technology bumper sticker on his truck and a Starfleet Academy sticker on Mom's van, yet he still, not even in jest, accepts the title of Nerd. But he spawned me. There's nerd blood in those veins, whether he wants to admit it or not.

Mom, on the other hand, was always a bit more willing to be open about her nerdier side. She could have stopped Dad from branding her van with the mark of a couple of huge nerds, but she didn't. They both thought it was awesome.

Our mutual raging-nerd factors aside, we were a very ordinary young family. As far as a kid's life goes, things were good. I had friends, and I had a cool little sanctuary in my house to camp out in and play with my toys and video games and watch movies all the time. Things couldn't be better. But Mom and Dad knew the real score: things were going to change soon.

For the sake of preserving the very fabric that made up those many blissful afternoons, they kept what a six-year-old would consider to be the ugly, awful truth to themselves as long as they could: we were going to move away from Lynn.

I distinctly remember two very polar emotions about moving. On the one hand, I remember the overwhelming feeling of "Whoa! Cool!" when Dad showed me the plans he had drawn for our new house. He and my mom would spend countless hours in his office going over layouts, reshaping rooms, and contemplating the pros and cons of things like having the laundry room on the first floor as opposed to in the basement. While they pored over their dream house, I sat cross-legged in the next room playing *Marble Madness* on Nintendo, unaware of what exactly it meant to move. I didn't quite appreciate the gravity of the situation. My world had existed entirely within that neighborhood. Any trips we took—from short jaunts to relatives' houses and school or to the far reaches of Disney World—could only be the work of my parents' seemingly divine hands. Building a new house just seemed like a fun thing to hear my parents talk about or watch Dad do on weekends when we'd drive up to visit him at the site to bring him lunch. It was like that conversation you have with your friends about starting a band—a fun idea that no one ever intends to see through to fruition.

So that was one way I looked at our new house. The other feeling I had about moving was absolute contempt for my parents after we pulled in to what I was supposed to consider my new driveway, after I unpacked my toys in what I was supposed to call my new room, and Lynn and all I had ever known was, from then on, half an hour and a forever away.

CHAPTER 3

QUEEF AND ME, OR HOW I LEARNED TO START WORRYING AND LOVE STAR WARS

DESPITE THE FACT THAT ROWLEY, Massachusetts, looked more like Endor, it certainly had a lot in common with Tatooine. Like its location. Though it's just twenty-five miles north of Lynn, the half-hour trip always felt like it took hours. Rowley looked so unlike Lynn and the surrounding towns that it may as well have been in another state. It reminded me of New Hampshire, with lots of trees and highway stretches that never seemed to end. As I grew bigger, the town got smaller, and the highways didn't seem quite so long. Still, as a little kid who had just been uprooted from all he'd ever known, I was less than thrilled. Armed with a pack of Crayolas and some construction paper, I drew a map to the gas station and swore to my mom that I was going to ride my bike there, get directions back to Lynn, and live with my grandparents. She eventually talked me off the ledge, but life is hard for a kid in a new town. Kids are cruel and merciless, and given the choice between being seven again or bare-knuckle boxing a silverback gorilla to death for a mate, I'd have to go with the gorilla.

We moved in June, and things weren't all that bad right away. As luck would have it, a kid I had played soccer with in Lynn lived two houses down. Billy was a nice guy, and I thought I might be able to make a go of it and make a few new friends.

Billy soon introduced me to a pudgy, ever-squinting goofball whom everyone called Queef. I cannot do justice to the overwhelming horror I felt on the day, many years later, when I found out that a queef is in fact a reasonable facsimile of a fart that comes out of some nice lady's vagina. For years we all called this kid Queef. To his face, in front of our parents, you name the person, and we were squeaking "Queefs" out in front of them left and right. I asked my mother once why she never put a stop to it. She became very serious and said point blank, "When you're a parent, you tell me whether or not you want to have the pussy-fart conversation with your seven-year-old."

Queef, Billy, and I would hang out most afternoons, running through the trails behind our houses, getting Billy's little brother to eat things out of their dog's food dish, and talking our parents into driving us to the now long-defunct comics shop, Waxx Paxx, to buy Marvel Comics trading cards. On rainy days we'd play board games or sit in front of the TV playing Nintendo. One time we rented the Ewok movies, and I remembered having seen one of them in Disney World a couple of years before. My parents had gone out that night, needing some time away from my sister and me, if only for a few hours. A Disney-employed babysitter kept Amanda entertained and quiet while the TV did the same for me. She had plopped me in front of *Caravan of Courage* to watch in awe as the Ewoks and a couple of kids killed a giant spider and saved their parents. While watching the movie again with Billy and Queef on that rainy afternoon, I couldn't figure out why the scene where the humans and that hairy guy fought an octopus thing in a big pile of trash was missing; I had thought that the garbage scene in *A New Hope* was actually part of one of the Ewok flicks. Slowly my knowledge of the galaxy was starting to come into focus.

Second grade and a new school were just around the bend, and I was, for the time being, surprisingly content with the move. I had yet to meet the rest of the guys in the neighborhood, but one day, while Billy, Queef, and I were walking down the street toward Billy's, they intercepted us and made a hell of an introduction. They all jumped out of nowhere, armed to the teeth with heavy balls of mud and the occasional rock. There was no warning, no ominous feeling that we were walking into a trap. It was like when Han, Leia, and Chewie were escorted to dinner by Lando Calrissian only to come face-to-face with Vader and Boba Fett. We were just minding our own business, with no one to defend us, and by the time we realized some shit was going to go down, it was too late.

"Get 'em!" someone yelled from behind the trees. The rest was a blur.

The boys all popped up from behind whatever natural cover they were using to conceal themselves. Battle cries filled the air and were almost as plentiful as the projectiles that rained down upon us. Billy pulled a Lando, jumping behind the nearest mound and joining the attack. Queef and I just put up our hands to block our faces and ran. His house was closer, so that's where I sought refuge until it was safe for me to crawl back home, where Mom would introduce me to Star Wars. The days of our little trio were over. Not too long after the Incident, the two of them had quite a falling out.

"Hey, Billy," Queef called from just outside his garage before whipping a ball of dirt at his now-former friend.

"You're dead, Queef!"

Billy rushed him, taking him to the ground, shoving fistfuls of dirt and mud in his face and cursing up a storm. As quick as it started it was over. Billy marched off, leaving a filthy Queef to rot in the driveway while I watched in horror.

"Who cares," Queef sniffed. "We don't need that asshole anyway."

Billy had officially changed camps, opting to be a bully, though by no means as large a douchebag as the rest of them, and that's the way things went for the next few years. It was everyone else against Queef and me. Occasionally even Queef would take a dig at me if he thought it would help him save face in front of the other guys.

"Tony, I have something terrible to tell you," he said one day.

"What?"

"I don't know how to say this, but you're dead."

"Are you sure?"

"Positive. My grandfather is an exorcist. I know all the signs. For example," he put on one of those cheap little police helmets you buy at the arcade with twenty Skee-Ball tickets, "I can only see you when I flip this visor down."

"Come on, I'm not dead. Am I?"

"Oh, visor's up. Where'd you go?"

"Shut up."

"Visor's down. I see you again. Want proof? I can tell you what you're wearing, but if I do, you have to help me talk to other dead people."

I always got over stunts like this because it never saved him from being dumped on for very long—the two of us were stuck in the same boat. Queef, for all intents and purposes, was a punch line for all the bullies who lived in our neighborhood, and to be perfectly honest, he did it to himself. He would come up with ridiculous claims and defend them to the end. Queef regaled us with stories of living in Indiana, where this one time he was attacked by a ravenous swarm of killer bees, or the time he was kidnapped and then rescued by his dad, a master black belt in kung fu. He rode a jaundice-colored Huffy that was "built from scrap parts," and his uncles included the likes of Larry Bird and Indiana Jones, a lie he thought no one would see through because he was the only one of us who had ever lived in Indiana.

"And you know my grandfather, well, one of them anyway, he invented the Ewoks!" went another one of his tall tales.

"Shut up, Queef!" one of the bullies would order before giving him a hard upwards karate chop to the junk, a move referred to in hushed, terrified whispers as the Ric Flair.

"No! Guys, really," he insisted, nursing his battered crotch. "He made those Ewok movies, swear to God!"

Later on, when it was just the two of us sitting on the swing set in his backyard, I confronted him about it. The prospect of knowing the grandson of the guy who "invented" the Ewoks was too sweet a temptation to resist.

"Did your grandfather really make those movies?" I asked.

"Why would I make that up?" Why indeed.

It was as if the blatant lies and exaggerations that spewed out of his mouth were guided missiles that were programmed to seek out the nearest jerk and blow up in his ear. With Queef around, I always had someone to play with and the bullies always had someone who made their jobs easier by constantly giving them new ammunition. In the neighborhood hierarchy there were two castes: everyone else and, below them, me and Queef. Even the guys' little brothers picked on us. But no matter what, when Queef was around, he seemed to get the brunt of it. Meanwhile, I watched, terrified, and never said a word for fear of what they'd do to me.

What always gets me when I look back at those days is that we all hung out all the time. The bullies and us two losers. That's just the way things were until we were old enough to ride our bikes across town. Then we were able to pick and choose the kids we rolled with and where we rolled. Until then it was an unstable brotherhood of proximity. At least after seeing *Empire* I had another world to call my own. I'd watch the movie and let it take me somewhere else, someplace where there wasn't any name-calling or dirt being hurled at my face. Characters like Chewbacca became the best friends I didn't have in the real world, and Luke's unwavering determination was my moral center. As the summer ended, the moment I had been dreading since we moved to Rowley had at last arrived. I was locked in the tractor beam of a brand-new year at a brand-new school that loomed menacingly ahead of me, not like a moon, but like a space station.

CHAPTER 4

I HAVE A BAD FEELING
ABOUT THIS . . .

SECOND GRADE STARTED ABOUT AS well as I had expected. In Robbie I found the first bully who targeted me specifically and was more malicious than mischievous in his tactics. While the familiar neighborhood bullies were less than pleasant, they still let me hang around and invited me over when one of them got a new Sega game or something they wanted to show off. They just ragged on me because I was the new kid or because Queef wasn't around. But this kid, this fat, mountain of a kid named Robbie, was out for blood. Years later the name Robbie still repulses me. This kid was a monster.

"Move," he growled at me from the bottom of the slide during one of my first recesses at Pine Grove Elementary. His voice was coated with a thick syrup of some sort of primordial and entirely inexplicable hate for me. I had, before this moment, never looked at the kid, never mind spoken to him.

"I can't," I pleaded. "There's someone else in front of me."

"I. Said. Move!"

He grabbed my pants by the waist and ripped me off of the ladder, throwing me to the ground like I was as useless to him as soap or a fresh piece of fruit. Stepping down off the ladder, he proceeded to pound me. He punched like a girl, something that would have been laughable if there hadn't been so much weight behind each limp-fisted swing. His cold, clammy hands felt like boxing gloves made out of deli meats, making the whole ordeal a very special kind of uncomfortable.

He never even went down the slide. My ass-kicking was all for naught.

My parents and Robbie's would be in and out of countless meetings with teachers and the principal over the years. While my mother pleaded on my behalf and my father foamed like a mad dog who had yet to lose his sense of where his loyalties lay, Robbie's folks sat there and defended him to the bitter end.

"He threw our son off the slide," Mom presented as exhibit A.

"If that fucked-up little cretin lays one more hand on my boy's head, I'll kill him myself!" Dad continued, his threat to execute a seven-year-old all but ignored. Everyone except the kid's parents would have paid to watch.

"Robbie doesn't mean to be so categorically evil," they'd insist of their amorphous little pile of chocolate-stained terror incarnate. "He's just misunderstood."

There was no misunderstanding on my end. I cowered in his sweaty shadow. No explanation they'd offer of his mental instability ever satisfied my parents or made me hate him any less. As far as I was concerned, he made my life hell, and my business was not forgiveness. My business was suppressing hatred, holding grudges, and keeping a mental list of all those who'd wronged me so that one day when I was the next George

Lucas I could send them all expensive-looking gift baskets stuffed to the gills with "Go Fuck Yourself." Fighting back was never an option. I was small and weak, and my allies ranged in number from no higher than a few to, more realistically, in the ballpark of zero. Even girls made fun of me. I was an island unto my prepubescent self.

During second-grade story time I'd draw pictures of AT-AT walkers and dream that one was stomping Robbie into Hoth's frozen tundra while the kid next to me, Jason, drew out plans for booby-trapping his house like Kevin in *Home Alone.* If my idols were Han Solo and Chewbacca, his were Bart Simpson and Macaulay Culkin. But before we could share any of those pop-culture fascinations with one another, the Teenage Mutant Ninja Turtles served as our conversational icebreaker.

"Hey, did you see *Ninja Turtles II?*" I asked one day when I spotted a Raphael toy in his backpack.

"Only eighteen times."

Those "heroes in a half-shell" had filled both of our toy boxes well beyond capacity and were the thing that got us talking in the first place. And talking. And talking. And talking. . . .

"Katana swords or nunchucks?" Jason asked.

"Bo staff," I answered without a moment's hesitation.

"That wasn't part of the question!"

"Why not? What's wrong with Don's bo staff?"

"Boys! I'm not going to tell you again. Stop. Talking. Now." Our second-grade teacher, Ms. Duncan, had to shut us up more times than she'd have cared to on any given day. After second grade we would be placed in separate classrooms until junior high. "It's a conspiracy," we'd say once we learned the word. "They're keeping us apart on purpose!"

We talked Star Wars too, despite how little of it we had seen at that point. One particularly cold day shortly before Christmas vacation sticks out in my mind, both because of its warm, fuzzy innocence and because it was the first of hundreds of lengthy Star Wars chats we'd have over the years. As we walked and talked our way through the playground, we pondered one of the many mysteries Lucas had laid out for us.

"Why's it say 'A long time ago' at the beginning?" Jason asked. "I thought science fiction was in the future."

I had often asked myself the same thing. I had assumed that since it was all set in a galaxy far, far away that their technology was leaps and bounds ahead of ours. Even so, it couldn't have taken place that long ago.

"Like, how long ago was it?" he wondered.

"I dunno. I think maybe it was during the time of the Pilgrims," I said.

"Then why didn't the Pilgrims come over in the *Falcon* or something? If other people were using spaceships, then what was their excuse?" He was daring me to come up with a good answer.

"They live in another galaxy, dude—they probably stopped using boats millions of years ago. I bet Earth didn't even have dinosaurs yet when they were still using boats."

Yeah, that sounded about right.

With Christmas vacation came the surge of youthful excitement that always accompanies a week off from school and an impending shower of new toys. For me the excitement was doubled: this would be my first solid break from Robbie's attacks on my easily bruised frame.

As I tore through the snowman-patterned wrapping paper, I checked off what I had and had not received from my list to Santa. I was never a greedy kid, knowing full well that Mr. Claus had a lot of stops to make and barely enough time to make all of the necessary preparations. In an effort to maximize efficiency and make the Jolly One's life as easy as possible, my lists were succinct and detailed, but never overambitious. So color me surprised when, after I opened the LEGO kit and action figures I had asked for, I found a small, hefty present was left.

"Is it mine?" Amanda asked, immediately chucking whatever new doll she had in her hands at the prospect of something newer, even if it was only newer by a matter of minutes. "Give it to me if it's mine!"

"I don't think that one's for you," Mom said.

"Why not?"

"Hey, what's wrong with that Barbie you just had?" Dad asked.

"It's not Barbie! It's her sister, Skipper!"

"Yeah, whatever. Play with that."

Amanda folded her arms and fell back on her pink pile of Christmas presents. She picked up her doll and twisted its head around with a creepy, quiet intensity.

The mystery box was addressed to me. The shape and weight of this particular gift didn't match that of anything I had requested. I opened it slowly and with great caution. To this day I won't rush through the process of unwrapping a present I'm clueless about—and as a natural-born gift-snoop and one who still maintains a very strict wish list, there is little that will, or should, catch me off guard.

I peeled the paper back to reveal a black box, its packaging made to look as if a quick, neat hand had written a personal note on it. Further down were the faces of Yoda, Luke, the droids, and Princess Leia, all looking out at me and asking, "What took you so long?"

Like a Wookiee sensing that a smuggler to whom I owed a life-debt was in danger underneath all the smiling Frosties and Santas, I tore off the rest of the wrapping paper. I turned the box over and over in my hands as the words "Star Wars Trilogy" and the repeated images of each movie's box art really started to soak in. My heart began to race. I flipped the box back over to the fake-handwritten note printed on its back:

Fifteen years ago I set out to make a film for a generation growing up without fairy tales.

Star Wars was my own elaborate fantasy, but its popularity has gone beyond anything I had ever imagined.

In years to come I hope that you, your children, and your children's children will enjoy experiencing this saga as much as I have.

—George Lucas

I didn't even notice who the gift was from. Did Mom and Dad decide to finish what was started on that miserable July day when I saw *Empire* for the first time? Was Santa pulling an Obi-Wan Kenobi? Was he giving me these movies, my birthright as it had been written that night in my Dad's Toyota at the drive-in, just as Obi-Wan Kenobi had given Luke his father's lightsaber? It didn't matter. For all I cared, George Lucas himself had given it to me personally. It was Wonka's Golden Ticket. It was an all-access pass to the one place I really wanted to be and to see the only people who made me feel happy and safe. It was the greatest gift I have ever been given, and it was going to be put to use immediately.

I sat in a nest of shredded wrapping paper, still in my PJs and ignoring the mound of toys under the tree while I watched *Star Wars*. I probably didn't blink. If it weren't for the fact that company was going to be coming over later that day, I would have sat in that very spot until each of the tapes had been played. Instead I was pressured into eating a breakfast consisting mostly of candy, taking a shower, and putting on my dress clothes. Why I had to dress up in my own home I never understood, but that morning I didn't care. It was the only Christmas I can remember where I had to get dressed up and didn't fuss about it. When I came downstairs, the cheese and crackers were all laid out for company and the trash from opening presents had been swept away. While Mom and Dad were distracted with getting the rest of the house and my little sister ready for the day, I opted to skip *Empire* and go for some more unexplored territory. The first wave of guests arrived just in time to watch Luke slay Jabba the Hutt's rancor.

Watching *Star Wars* for the first time was an experience nearly identical to watching *The Empire Strikes Back*, with the only possible difference being that the occasional boredom I felt with Han and Leia's romance was nowhere to be found. In its place was overwhelming giddiness over the extra-terrestrial Noah's ark that is the Mos Eisley Cantina. Among the jazzy licks being laid down by Figrin D'an and the Modal Nodes, the otherworldly barflies, and Obi-Wan's dismembering grace with a lightsaber, I was pretty much the happiest kid in the world that Christmas.

It was amazing to finally see where all the characters I already knew so well came from and to watch the events that *Empire*'s text scroll hinted at unfold. Han was a total jerk, and sometimes not in that endearing way he was in *Empire*. He said it himself: he didn't care about the cause; he just wanted to get paid. I often felt like he genuinely didn't like anyone other than Chewbacca, but it didn't matter, because he was still supercool, and in the end he let his inner hero reveal itself. I could almost forgive him for giving Luke so much crap because Luke was kind of a brat sometimes. Everyone complains about whiny ol' Luke Skywalker, but at the time I appreciated that he was such a whiny kid. I could relate to that. It made me feel like maybe someday I could blow up a giant government super-weapon— a really, really cool super-weapon. It was stuff like seeing the Death Star finally realized and in action, Darth Vader's general presence, and that too-cool-for-school screechy howling noise the TIE fighters made when they dive-bombed the *Millennium Falcon* that made me so conflicted as a fan. I had to root for the good guys, especially in light of their own arsenal of cool, but it was tough to not want the Empire to succeed sometimes. Oppression, hate-mongering, and all-around evilness aside, they were pretty badass.

Return of the Jedi—which got popped in the VCR as soon as I had rushed through some pointless tasks like brushing my teeth and pulling on some socks that matched my stupid dress pants—was a bit of an anomaly. All of the three movies have their own distinct feel to them, but *Jedi* was like two movies in one. The first act, in Jabba's palace, took steps into a darker, seedier part of science fiction that I would remain otherwise ignorant about for some time. This was gangland. Sex, drugs, and murderous dogs were everywhere in that dank, smoky hell-hole. If Threepio and Artoo hadn't been there the whole time, it wouldn't even have felt like a Star Wars movie. It was all very alluring in a way that I hadn't yet experienced in this universe. For two movies now there had been references to Jabba the Hutt, but to finally see him, a disgusting Muppet embodiment of hedonism, was both awesome and terrifying. The Cantina seemed like a nonstop good time, even when guys were threatening Luke's life. In Jabba's palace there were no illusions about what happened within those walls. It was evil, a cesspool of intergalactic malcontents, and they were proud of it.

After the gang saved Han and left Tatooine, the movie was back to form, and we returned to familiar territory. I didn't mind at the time. If anything, finally seeing the attack on the first Death Star made me antsy to see some more space battles, and *Jedi* certainly delivered. Even the Ewoks seemed cool. I now feel fortunate for having thought that at a young enough age that even now, though I know that by all rights the Ewoks are actually kind of lame, I can still enjoy them. Watching Threepio tell the Ewok village of the adventures he'd had over the course of the first two movies was particularly awe inspiring that morning and it still holds a place in my heart as one of my favorite scenes in the series. I suppose it's because I felt like one of those midgets in teddy-bear pajamas, watching and listening with eyes and ears open wide as the amazing saga of Luke, Han, and Leia played out before me. If I hadn't known it before, I certainly knew it then: I was in love.

By the time Luke had stood his ground against the Emperor and Darth Vader finally saw the light that was so far down the tunnel of darkness, my hierarchy that would hold for several years had been set. *Return of the Jedi*, *Star Wars*, and *The Empire Strikes Back*, in that order, were my three favorite movies. The tapes themselves were my most prized possessions, and wherever I went, they were in tow. Inside the box was a list of the films' original release dates, directors, writers, box-office grosses, and award nominations and wins. I memorized it all. I also memorized every inch of Carrie Fisher's illustrated body on the covers of *Star Wars* and *Jedi*—her boobs lifted to kingdom come on the former and the obvious, sultry pose in her metal slave bikini on the latter.

I probably watched them all a couple more times before the Christmas vacation week was out. There's no doubting that Jason and I plowed through the trilogy at least once after building our own Echo Base in the giant snow pile next to my garage. There was a whole new world of understanding open to me after finally seeing the trilogy. It was one of pop culture's vital organs. It was Rome, with all roads leading to it, and I had at long last stepped out of the bush and onto the path. I had taken my first step into a larger world.

CHAPTER 5

I CAME, I SAW NOTHING, I WET MY PANTS

AFTER CHRISTMAS VACATION I RETURNED to school feeling a bit better about my situation. I was coasting on a high after finally seeing all three Star Wars movies. Things were going to be okay. As far as I knew, Jason and I were the only two kids who cared about Star Wars, which made the high even better. It felt like we had our own little secret. Star Wars was ours and ours alone, and it became the cinematic equivalent of a tree house, letting us sneak away and hide behind its walls from the world outside. Of course, life has a way of throwing some unexpected monkey wrenches your way once in a while, and that spring was no exception.

Our teacher, Ms. Duncan, had a treasure box, and when we did something of merit—such as solving a math problem correctly or reading a certain number of books in a month—we were allowed to pick a prize from it. One day early in the new

year I did something deserving, and for my prize I chose an
orange marker that smelled "exactly" like oranges. It was one
of the few non–Star Wars related instances I can recall when
I was genuinely happy during school that year. Everyone cov-
eted those markers—the ones that smelled just like the fruit
that they shared their color with. I pulled it from the box and I
felt like Luke taking his dad's lightsaber from Obi-Wan's hand
and lighting it up for the first time. *I'm going to use this*, I told
myself, *as soon as I get the chance.*

That chance came at story time. While Ms. Duncan paced
back and forth across the front of the room reading us a chapter from *James and the Giant Peach*, I sat hunched over my
desk, orange-smelling marker in hand, drawing a picture of
Bart Simpson. I could smell the sweet, citrusy aroma drifting
up from the paper. I didn't care that Bart was yellow. *Orange
is half yellow, damn it!* I heard myself telling imaginary critics and naysayers. *Eat it, fart knockers. It's my day! I won this
marker!* That was just it: getting that prize was like sticking it
to everyone else and I was loving every minute of it. Yet my
pride proved to be my undoing. As I sat there, drawing without a care in the world and listening to Roald Dahl's prose
dance out of my teacher's lips, a faceless foe crept up on me.
Without warning there was a quick tinge in my bladder, followed by a mocking feeling of relief in the form of a warm,
wet lap.

My body, hijacked by unknown forces, had chosen to wet
my pants without even offering me a chance to excuse myself
first. I was a spectator to my own self-induced humiliation.
Slowly my hand went up, trembling. I caught Ms. Duncan's eye.

"Yes?" she asked.

"Ms. Duncan, I had an accident."

My trance was broken by a Fourth of July, grand-finale fireworks display of laughter from a classroom full of seven- and eight-year-olds. Robbie's rumbling, phlegmy laugh, appropriately Jabba-esque, stood out among the noise. I imagined he was licking his chocolate-stained lips and wringing those wicked bouquets of breakfast links he called hands while he dreamt of giving the pants-wetter a flying suplex off of a jungle gym. Immediately my inner monologue started demanding answers, punctuating each question with a subconscious finger jab to the chest. *Why would you say that? What the hell's wrong with you? Couldn't you have just said you need to go to the nurse? That you don't feel good? You just signed your own damn death warrant in your own damn pee! If a Wookiee wore pants, you know that he wouldn't be lame enough to wet them, right? I hate you! I hate you! I hate myself!*

Jason was, aside from our teacher, the only person in the room who wasn't laughing.

"Sorry, dude," he offered sadly as I walked passed him.

Ms. Duncan stood waiting for me at the end of my row. She put her hand on my shoulder and walked me to the door, the laughter becoming muted as I receded further into a state of shock. She opened the door and pointed me in the direction of the nurse's office. I took that long walk down a short hallway and sat, sobbing, as I waited for the nurse to bring me a pair of Roger Rabbit Underoos, dry jeans with a stretchy waistband, and a plastic bag to put my soiled bottoms in. After I changed, she tried to comfort me: "Tony, don't cry. These things happen. . . . Now, would you please remember to have your mother wash the jeans and undies before you return them tomorrow?" I wanted to ask her what guarantee she was giving me that the last miserable little geek who'd peed his pants had washed the school's rental shorts. Instead I just hung my head, embarrassed that she even had to ask.

"Now, go back to class. Everything will be fine."

Nothing would be fine. Was she kidding me? Had she no kids of her own, or not ever been a child herself at one point? Could it be that she had been born an out-of-touch, premeno-pausal woman who never had to endure the gauntlet of suffering that is childhood? Nothing would be fine. No kid gets a pass on something like this, especially not the new kid. The words *I had an accident* would linger around me like an acrid, yellow fog for years.

A couple of months after "I had an accident" became the fastest-growing catchphrase to charm our nation since "Where's the beef?" a little movie called *Jurassic Park* suddenly popped up on our pop-culture radar. It lit the schoolyard on fire. Every boy was sucker-punched by the idea of seeing dinosaurs on the big screen. It took over our imaginations. It tore down social walls. It was then, before the dawn of a new Jurassic era, that everyone got along because of a single, common goal: to see that movie as soon as it came out.

My folks seemed just as excited. My old man went out, bought the book, and read through it in what seemed like just a few hours. My mom pointed out that it was directed by Steven Spielberg, a name I recognized from its association with *Back to the Future* and *E.T.*, something that only further fueled my lust for this movie. Then she did herself one better by pointing out that Spielberg and George Lucas were best buds and suggested I go digging through the boxes of videos for something called *Raiders of the Lost Ark*.

One afternoon there was a "making of" special on TV showing how they were going to bring thunder lizards to life, and I made another connection. Industrial Light & Magic were doing the effects for *Jurassic Park*, and the name, like Spielberg, turned on a light bulb of recognition. I popped in one of my Star Wars videos and fast-forwarded to the end credits to see the name Industrial Light & Magic as those responsible for X-Wings and Death Stars. After watching that special I didn't want to be George Lucas anymore; I wanted to be one of the guys who rigged the explosives and squibs, who designed and redesigned and re-redesigned the look of a movie. I wanted to work at ILM, the North Pole of special-effects studios, where Santa George and his helper elves worked tirelessly for all the good boys and girls in movie land. But before I did anything else, I needed to see *Jurassic Park*.

As the release date neared, I started drooling like a hungry T-rex eyeing a wounded triceratops. I started dreaming about it, talking about it as if I'd already seen it.

"Oh! And that part on the commercial when the dinosaur flips over the truck? How cool was that?"

"You know that this is going to be the greatest movie of our lives, right?" Jason asked.

"Man, if I don't see that movie soon I'm probably going to wet my pants again! Um . . . please don't tell anyone that I said that."

Unfortunately when the reviews started coming in, they tipped my mother off to something she hadn't thought of before, despite it being one of the things I was most looking forward to about the movie: the dinosaurs ate people.

"You're not seeing that movie. It's too violent," she told me one night after a little-league game where Jason and I had just spent the better part of the game on the bench geeking out while our dads solidified plans for all of us to go see the movie that following weekend.

"The dinosaurs eat people. Did you know that? I thought it was going to be more like *E.T.*!" She said it with a whine in her voice that would have annoyed Marge Simpson, a pleading variation of Mother knows best. In this case she didn't. More like *E.T.*? Was she high? Her saying yes before considering the possibility that some poor sap or several would be torn awesomely asunder by the razor-sharp teeth and claws of, you know, dinosaurs, was no problem of mine. I begged. I got on my knees and groveled at the feet of the woman who was gracious enough to bestow upon me the gift of Star Wars but was so wicked a deity as to take away what could possibly be the next best thing. As far as I knew there was never going to be a chance for me to see *Star Wars* at the movies. *Jurassic Park* was going to be as good as it got.

As hard as I pleaded, there was no changing her mind. The great Oz had spoken in what she thought was my best interest. My mother, bless her and damn her in the same breath, actually thought I'd be scared of the dinosaurs. Dinosaurs! The stuff that—after Wookiees and lightsabers—her little boy's dreams were made of! There wasn't going to be anything on that screen that I hadn't already seen in my imagination or acted out with toy dinosaurs in the backyard. In her attempts to keep me safe from the horrors of cinematic achievement, she forgot what brought me joy: unbridled dino-carnage.

Opening weekend came and went. On Monday school was alive with the electric charge of a few hundred boys who saw the coolest damned thing to grace the silver screen in their short lifetimes. Despite a *Jurassic Park* T-shirt and the few action figures that I was able to acquire, my attempts to hide the fact that I hadn't seen the movie proved to be a fool's errand. At the very least I got off without being chastised for missing the movie that had been billed as "65 Million Years in the Making." Instead I was pitied. Like someone with a horrible disease or disfigurement, I was met with the kindest, most patronizing words, but when my back was turned I heard the whisperings of what a poor, wretched soul I was.

"Did you see *Jurassic Park*?" someone would ask a friend.

"Shh! Pee Pants's mom won't let him see it."

"Oh no . . ."

"Yeah, so keep it down. You don't want to be the one they say pushed him to suicide, do you?"

I may as well have packed up and moved to a pop-culture leper colony. Thankfully, summer vacation was a couple of short weeks away. At least over the summer any reminder of what I'd been missing would be nothing more than a TV spot here and there. Meanwhile, the movie would continue to rake in millions from the moms all across America who loved their sons enough to take them back for second and third viewings. Comforting me was the knowledge that just as Jacob Marley had to drag a chain forged of his own misdeeds through the afterlife, my mother would probably have to push a wheelbarrow full of *Jurassic Park*'s box-office receipts around when she wound up in whatever circle of hell they have reserved for parents who deprive their kids of such important, awesome things.

CHAPTER 6

INDIANA SKYWALKER
AND THE RECTUM OF DOOM

"WHY DO YOU HAVE A Band-Aid on your eye?" classmates asked me often during those first miserable couple of weeks of third grade. "It's not a Band-Aid. It's an eye patch," I replied, defending my badge as the sheriff of Geektown, USA. Thanks to a lazy left eye, I now not only had to wear glasses, but also I had an eye patch for a couple of months as well. Not a cool, pirate eye patch, but rather a skin-toned adhesive pad that I slapped over my good eye to strengthen the bad one. The result was an eyebrow that looked like it was being poorly plucked on a daily basis.

"Yeah, well it looks like a Band-Aid."

I imagine that if pirates had worn such lame-looking eye patches, they wouldn't have been nearly as feared and admired as history has made them out to be. In fact, the tables probably would have been completely turned.

"Arg! Avast ye scurvey dogs, we be here for yer wenches and yer gold!"

"Nah," a snickering British admiral would have responded, "how about you just give us your lunch money and swing back to your shanty boat before we beat your ass down, cyclops."

Making matters even worse was the fact that my peripheral vision was totally crippled on my right side. Several embarrassing bumps, run-ins, and trips over things that were right in front of me left me doing a constant, Artoo head swivel to get a good scan of my surroundings. It was degrading crap like this that made me feel like having glasses was more of a handicap than not having them. Corrected vision be damned. At that moment the grief I got for having a big, shiny bull's-eye slapped on my face far outweighed any good it did me later on.

"*Star Trek?* You actually watch that crap?" Tom sneered.

It was story-writing time in third grade, a time when I liked to steal the successful ideas of others and just barely make them my own. One of my first mash-ups was a not-so-clever love child of *Star Trek* and *Seaquest: DSV*—not-so-cleverly entitled *Sea Trek*.

"Um, yeah, 'cause it's awesome." I confessed to following both of the shows religiously, and to flat-out loving Star Wars, outing myself as a sci-fi nerd. Tom's disgust over how sorry an excuse of a human being I was became palpable.

"You know that, right? You're like, the biggest nerd in the room. I bet you don't even watch *Saved By the Bell*, do you?"

"What's that?"

"Are you retarded?"

"No?"

"It's, like, the best show ever! It's what all us cool kids watch!" Seriously. He said that. This was a kid who would prove to be the same kind of cool as a rusty, mid-eighties Camaro painted primer coat gray, complete with a bottomless trunk that was perpetually filled to the brim with warm Keystone Light.

Nevertheless, I went home that afternoon and decided to give it a try. It sucked. *Saved By the Bell* just sucked. I was eight, maybe nine years old, and that crap had no meaning to me. Why should I have cared about older kids doing older-kid things? Zack and Slater were the types of guys who would probably stuff me into a locker, so I found no one to relate to, aside from the show's resident spaz-slash-Poindexter, Screech, but even he rubbed me the wrong way. He should have just kept his mouth shut and his head down and cut his losses, but instead he seemed to always go out of his way to make himself an easy target. Forget Lisa, dude, it's never gonna happen. Calm down, shut your cake hole, and stick to playing with computers and watching scrambled porn. As a third-grader I had no business with that show. I knew it. The show knew it. But "everyone" watched it. I just didn't get it, and I knew that there wasn't something there that Tom was picking up on and I was missing. None of us had any frame of reference for problems with dating, detention, cars, or curfews. We were nine.

So, of course, at school the next day I lied through my teeth.

"Hey, Tom, did you watch *Saved By the Bell* last night?" I said coolly, or at least how I thought cool sounded. The truth was in my eye and written all over my eye patch. I had no idea what I was talking about.

"Yeah, I did. Did you?"

"Uh, yeah! It was only the coolest thing ever, just like you said! That kid, you know, that cool one. . . ."

"Slater?"

"Yeah, Slater. He like, said 'Time out!' and everything stopped and then—"

"Oh, you mean Zack."

"What?"

"Zack does the time out."

"Oh yeah, that's what I meant. Zack did that, and that was so awesome." Tom looked at me with newfound contempt. It was bad enough that I was a nerd, but now I was a nerd trying not to be. I was a pathetic life form who was well beyond any form of pity.

"Dude, he does that like every episode." He shook his head disapprovingly, and as he walked away, he threw one last insult my way: "Maybe you should just stick to stupid things, like Star Wars."

After that I kept my true love of nerdier forms of entertainment secret from anyone who didn't share my beliefs. I started claiming that *Jaws* was my favorite movie, a believable lie because while it wasn't number one, it was easily in my top ten. No one would contest it, because what's cooler than sharks ripping unsuspecting beachgoers to shreds? Plus, Jason and I were pretty deep into our *Jaws* phase at that point. So deep in fact, that we were known to write the names of our favorite characters on our sandwiches with condiments.

"Hey," Jason would say, pointing at his open-faced turkey and cheese, "look what I did." He had written "Quint" in spicy brown mustard.

"Cool!" I had written "Jaws Jr." on mine. We were under the impression that the shark in *Jaws 2* was the first shark's kid.

Fourth grade rolled around, and while Jason and I had grown closer—we were at each other's houses so often that his little cousin started to think that I was a relative he had never been told about—the fact that we weren't in class together made most of any given school day harder than it needed to be. Thankfully, in that first month of the new school year, I finally found a new in-class buddy in David, another like-minded kid with a soft spot for the nerdier things in life.

"What are you drawing?" David asked me, spying the colored pencil doodle of Boba Fett I was trying to hide.

"Nothing."

"Come on, is that the bounty hunter from *The Empire Strikes Back*?"

I took off my glasses and eyed him carefully. How did I know he wasn't a spy, a cool wolf in geek's clothing? I risked exposing myself anyway.

"Yeah, it is."

"Cool. I like drawing too."

He showed me a bunch of drawings from his art folder, a bunch of mutants and freaks inspired by covers of comics like *The Amazing Spider-Man* and *WildC.A.T.s.* He was good, very good, in fact, and I was instantly jealous.

"Whoa," I practically drooled, "these are awesome."

"Thanks. I like your Boba Fett, too, but his feet look a little weird. Want me to show you how I draw feet?"

Before I knew it I had a new friend. Like, a friend-friend, and not just someone to talk to in class or during lunch. David and I formed a bond rooted firmly in sci-fi fare that included superheroes and Star Wars. *Batman: The Animated Series* was a mutually shared after-school religious obligation, and stuff like

Stargate and Alec Baldwin's goofy though fondly remembered turn as a pulp vigilante in *The Shadow* became instant classics in our eyes. We watched them often, and usually back to back, at sleepovers fueled by the TV's blue light, Doritos, and as much soda as our stomachs and bladders would retain. Hanging out meant geeking over movies and computer games, occasionally talking about girls we liked but knew would never speak to us.

"What if she's the girl for me?" I'd pine after the lights went out and we watched as the glow-in-the-dark planet stickers stuck to the ceiling slowly started to lose their luster. "What if she's the girl I'm supposed to be with but I blow it because she doesn't even know I exist."

"Who cares, dude. We're not even ten yet. Besides, she's got more of a moustache than that kid on my bus who says he started shaving last month."

"Yeah, but it's a cute moustache, isn't it?"

It didn't matter all that much to me whether any of my frequently changing prepubescent crushes would never talk to me in a million years. I was just happy to have a whopping two friends.

But even with friends, it was tough to stay optimistic about life when jackals with bad bowl cuts were prowling my street. The guys in the neighborhood were still as bad as ever, if not worse. Their older brothers had moved on to junior high, so they'd taken it upon themselves to pick up the slack and keep Queef and me in our places.

One snowy midwinter's day an impromptu snowball fight broke out at the bus stop and sure as shit my complete lack of basic motor skills bit me right in the ass.

"Look at him!" one of the guys yelled from across the street. "He can't even clear the road!"

As I hurled snowballs with all the accuracy, speed, and overall gayness of a little girl, the laughing just got louder and louder. Soon they were taunting me to throw more, prodding menacingly at my fractured pride.

"Whoa! Watch the heat on that one, guys!"

"There's smoke comin' off that pitch!"

"Easy, Nolan, we still got a few innings left after this one!"

And just like that a seemingly throwaway insult became the new nickname that would haunt me for the foreseeable future. After the snowball fight had ended—even after the snow had melted, the seasons changed, and the snow came back again—the name stuck, a twisting blade covered in the salt of a reminder that my feelings were expendable and my miserable existence was proof that if God did exist, he was kind of a douchebag too. The fact that Nolan Ryan was such a superstar ballplayer that I didn't have to ask my dad who Ryan was somehow made it even worse. They were mocking me with sports. What cold-hearted bastard tipped these creeps off to irony?

A few days later I approached the bus stop cautiously. Mom was half a street behind me practically dragging my little sister behind her by the ankle, an early warning sign suggesting that as she got older, Amanda would only become more obnoxious about having to be bothered with school. When I got to the corner I tried to stand as far away from the guys as possible without looking like I was trying to hide from them. Behind me I heard the quick crunching of running feet in the snow. Chris came up behind me and slapped me in the back of the head.

"Morning, Nolan!" Whack!

The guys all laughed and then went back to ignoring me, but something inside me wasn't going to take it anymore. Some strange, deluded section of my brain thought it would actually be a good idea to stand up for myself. Without even pausing to give it a second thought I walked up behind Chris, smacked him in the back of the head and demanded, "How do you like it, asshole?" I barely finished the question before I was facedown in the dirty snow getting whaled on.

"You think you're cool now, Nolan? Huh?!"

All I could hear above me was the "Fwomp! Fwomp!" of Chris's gloved fists punching my heavy winter coat. All around us was a chorus of laughter, and beyond that was my mother's shrieking. She ran over to break it all up. Had this been a movie, I might have been the one on the winning end of the fight as opposed to being stuck on the ass end of the ass-kicking. Hell, if this had been a movie, I would have at least earned a degree of street cred. "Hey man," Chris or one of the other guys would say to me later that day, "I still don't like you, but now I respect you." No dice. All I did was prove what they all thought: if forced into a fight, I went down easy and depended on my mother to save the day.

Surprisingly, kids in my class seemed to be getting slightly—oh, ever so slightly—more amicable. By the time our fourth-grade winter vacation had come and gone, I had finally outlasted my new-kid phase, had paid my grade-school dues, and was no longer the nerdiest kid in class, at least not compared to the kid who thought that Power Rangers were real. Still, I didn't exactly do a lot to help my situation. A word to the wise: never think that ESP is something you can bring to show-and-tell.

"What's that?" someone asked as I stood at the front of the class where it was assumed I would be demonstrating some skill or talent I had.

"It means extra sensory perception. My mom says we have it!" Ugh.

"Prove it, Nolan!"

I balled my fists up, bit down on my lip, and began to focus so hard that I thought I was going to shit my pants. The latent psychic in me called out across the astral plane to Mom, Dad, Mel Brooks, General Patton's ghost, anybody. I was dying up in the spotlight, brazen enough to claim I had an awesome super-power like telepathy but with none of the actual superpowers to back it up.

I opened one eye slowly, looking out at the hanging jaws, the snickering faces, and a teacher who was mortified for me. I had to think of something, needed some sort of excuse as to why my heightened mental capabilities were temporarily rendered useless.

"Come on, Nolan, can you call your mom with your brain or not?"

"I . . . uh, well I can, but not right now. There must be some sort of psychic interference."

I trudged to my seat to an imagined soundtrack of crickets playing sad trombones. If looks could give wedgies, I'd have been picking my briefs out of my butt crack for a week. My classmates couldn't even laugh. They had no idea how to compute what I had just tried and failed to do with such fervent sincerity.

Psychic gymnastics aside, I wasn't necessarily digging my hole deeper that year. An in-class writing assignment was my first itty-bitty baby step in the right direction, but it was a total freak accident. If I had planned to write the shit out of what would typically be considered a throwaway assignment, I'd have been some sort of junior evil mastermind. Or it wouldn't have worked at all. Such is the unpredictable alchemy of blind luck and a child's love of words like *anus*.

"Class, today we're going to combine our science and writing periods so you can write a creative story about how the digestive system works," Mrs. Salley instructed. "Try to have fun with it."

After I had turned in my story, she practically skipped to my desk and asked me to read my story to the class. Apparently Mrs. Salley had been bowled over by the mastery I displayed over the written word and my clock-like comedic precision when it came to poop jokes in a little story I called "Indiana Skywalker and the Rectum of Doom."

"Tony, this is very, very funny. I would love it if you would read this out loud to everyone."

"Uh. . . ."

Before I could tell her that, no, I was not about to get in front of the class and give everyone another reason to think I sucked, she had hoisted me up out of my seat.

"Everyone, Tony has written a very funny story for his digestive-system assignment, and I would like you all to give him your undivided attention while he reads it."

She looked down at me with no idea of the unspeakable horror she had just unleashed on me.

"Go ahead, Tony."

"I . . . I don't . . ." I looked to her desperately and whispered, "I really don't want to do this."

"Oh, come on. It's funny! Just read it."

"No, really, maybe you could—"

"Tony. Just read it."

As the room started to spin, I raised the shaking piece of paper in my hand up to my face and tried to get my eyes, brain, and mouth to synch up and muscle through it.

"A long time ago in a mouth far, far away. . . ." Pop! I exploded. My fears all mounted into an all-out nuclear core meltdown, and I exploded in front of everybody.

"I can't do it!" I cried through rushing tears. "Don't make me read it, please. I just can't do it!"

Mrs. Salley had no idea what had just happened. Her attempt to help a weird little kid come out of his shell had backfired. Based on my reaction, she probably thought that she had just sentenced me to years of therapy.

"Okay, it's . . . shhh, no, stop. It's fine. Just, uh, go stand out in the hall, okay? I'll read it."

I ran out of the room and sat in the hallway, bawling my pathetic little eyes out. Back in the classroom Mrs. Salley read my story for me. Just as she had predicted, everyone thought it was hilarious. Even though they had mocked my now-debunked telepathy or given me grief about getting a pair of Reebok Pumps a year and a half after they were cool, they laughed with me when, for the first time, something I had written was shared with them. I couldn't believe it. "Indiana Skywalker and the Rectum of Doom" was the surprise hit of the 1994–95 school year, and I was missing it. I had been so afraid of being laughed at again that I had blown a chance to win the adoration and hearts of my peers. After she had finished reading it and put everyone back to work, she came and poked her head out into the hall.

"Are you okay now?"

I sniffed a booger back up into my nose, wiped my eyes and nodded in the affirmative, then shuffled back to my seat and waited for the standing ovation to start. Didn't they want to show a little appreciation for the comedic gem I just rocked their worlds with? Did I imagine the laughter that roared out at me from behind closed doors? The spotlight eluded me, and it was just as well. I probably would have peed my pants again if I had walked into a room full of cheering fans.

"Indiana Skywalker and the Rectum of Doom" became one of those mythic *did we or did we not make that up?* things in my house over the years. My teacher read it again at parents' night, where it was just as well received. It was all an excuse for jokes about the anus: what's not to like? But somewhere between the shortsighted days of my youth and the present, the story was lost.

"It's not the sort of thing I would have thrown away," my mom insisted. "If you wrote something called 'The Rectum of Doom' when you were nine, what kind of parent would I be if I didn't keep it?"

Our desperate search—which included but was not limited to ripping up floorboards, hiring bounty hunters, and writing a letter to my fourth-grade teacher—proved to be in vain. Eighteen years after I wrote the story, as we sat at the kitchen table drowning our defeat in pharmaceutical-grade spirits and pondering over any final possibilities for where the story might be, Amanda—deus ex machina—walked into the room and declared: "We have it on tape. I just watched it last week."

Amanda has always had what I considered to be an annoying fascination with watching old home movies. She could sit on the living room floor for hours, burning through stacks of videotapes without once blinking an eye. Unlike me, Amanda liked to watch us as little kids. All I ever got out of seeing those old tapes was a whiff of rancid nostalgia, a reminder of how grumpy and miserable I was during parts of my childhood.

"Shut the hell up!" I demanded.

"No, seriously, it's upstairs on a stack of tapes."

My mother and I looked at each other, stunned, and then raced up into the toy room with Amanda right on our heals, spewing venom at me for the years of shit I had given her for watching those stupid home movies. What follows is the complete, unabridged "Indiana Skywalker and the Rectum of Doom" as read by Mrs. Salley at parent-teacher night, on February 8, 1995.

A long time ago in a mouth far, far away lived Indiana Skywalker, world famous rectumologist. He was working on his TIE explorer when his friend Ham Solo came over.

"Hey, Indy, you home?" Ham shouted.

"Yeah, what do you want?" Indy shouted back.

"Imperial Poison Troops are attacking the digestive system!" Ham screamed.

"Be down in a minute," Indy told him.

He hopped in his TIE explorer and flew down to get Ham.

"Hop in," Indy said.

"Let's go save digestion," Ham said.

They were leaving the mouth and entering the esophagus.

"Oh no," Indy said in a worried voice.

"What?" Ham yelled.

"The epiglottis isn't shutting! We're going down the wrong pipe! Ahh!" Indy screamed.

"Hurry! Jump to light speed!" Ham said.

"Yes, we made it," Indy said calmly.

"Look in the stomach," Indy said.

"Yeah, those troops are freezing the enzymes and stopping the muscles from churning. None of the food will break down," Ham said.

"Lets fire the proton torpedoes and melt the frozen enzymes," Indy said, ready to fire.

"Fire!" Ham screamed.

Indy fired. The torpedoes blew up the troops and melted the enzymes.

"Good. Digestion flowing fine here," Indy said in relief.

Indy and Ham were leaving the stomach and entering the small intestine when all of the sudden . . .

"Oh no," Ham said.

"What? More troops?" Indy asked.

"No! Bile and pancreatic juices!"

"Oh! I'm too young to be digested!" Indy cried.

"Go! Go! Don't stop here or anyplace in the small intestine, because if you stop, we'll go through the villi and flow into the blood-stream," Ham told him.

So they kept going and going and going until they got to the large intestine.

"We're almost there, Indy. After this the digestive system will be free from the Poison Empire," Ham said excitedly.

"Why did we have to come this way? We would have traveled a lot faster through the bloodstream," Indy complained.

"Indy, move! Go! Go! Step on it!" Ham yelled.

Indy hit 1,000 miles per hour and raced through the large intestine. A big ball of waste was right behind him as he entered the rectum.

"Well, here we are, the main source—all the food poisoning in the rectum," Ham said.

"Wow, Ham, look at that. It's a huge ball of food poisoning," Indy said, staring at the blob.

"Hey, I know how to stop this thing," Ham said.

"How?" Indy asked.

"Your proton torpedoes. Those should kill the blob and unclog the anus," Ham said.

Indy fired the torpedoes, killed the blob, and digestion worked correctly from then on.

The end.

The ending seems a bit rushed. I also can't tell if my characters are inconsistent or if I was going for something along the lines of that classic "bumbling, incompetent hero who gets all the credit for his underappreciated, competent sidekick's work" routine. Third-act problems and questionable character actions aside, I think my writing career peaked when I was nine.

CHAPTER 7

PROOF OF AN EXPANDED UNIVERSE

"WELL," DAD BARKED ONE DAY at the end of baseball season as he angrily switched the radio from AM sports radio to FM classic rock, "the friggin' Bum Sox did it again!"

"Who?" I had slipped into a sports-radio-induced coma.

"The goddamned Red Sox!"

"What?"

"They just lost! Again!" He simmered for a minute then let out a sigh heavy with a season's worth of disappointment. "And now they're out of the playoffs."

"Huh?"

"Weren't you listening to the game?" I was so spaced out that I couldn't think of my own name for another ten minutes, never mind be able to talk about what we were listening to on the radio.

To say that I played sports as a kid would be a morbidly offensive overstatement. Aside from a rare couple of well-executed, fluke plays, I didn't so much play sports as I filled out rosters and took up a spot on the bench. Even after years of playing soccer, by the time I was ten I still had zero concept of how the game worked on a fundamental level. As far as baseball went, I was generally sequestered to what you might call the outer-rim section of the outfield.

Yet as uncoordinated and unathletic as I was, I was even worse at watching sports. I could rattle off the title scrolls for all three Star Wars movies and give you the name of every background character, but keeping up with just one inning of a Red Sox game on TV was, at the very least, a Herculean task of impossible proportions. This proved to be a bit of a roadblock when it came to talking to my father. Dad could talk about sports all day with someone who was interested, but talking to me about the Bruins or the Sox was about as conversationally stimulating as discussing batting averages and free agents with a ketchup packet. He tried anyway.

Likewise, I would try to talk to him about Star Wars, something I knew he liked on some level, but Dad didn't look at movies the way I did.

"I wonder what Ponda Baba and Dr. Evazan did to get the death sentence on twelve systems," I'd ponder aloud while we worked on model kits.

"Who are you talking to?"

"Oooh, or what Lando's maneuver at the Battle of Taanab was. Or, you know, what the Battle of Taanab was."

"I think this glue is getting to you. Do we need to open more windows?"

"Geez, Dad, it's all from Star Wars!"

"I don't remember those parts."

For him, movies were just a sweet couple of hours where he didn't have to worry about grown-up stuff. When the credits rolled, the movie ended, and bills, work, and fatherhood clocked back in. I threw myself wholeheartedly into fictional worlds. Movies would play in my head on an infinite loop. They never ended. They couldn't.

One Saturday afternoon late in 1995, Dad popped his head up into the toy room during a commercial break from a Bruins game. I was sitting amidst a pile of LEGOs and staring like a zombie into the colorful world of *Sonic the Hedgehog 2*.

"You almost done?" he asked.

I grunted an answer that could be interpreted as a yes.

"You want to go to the bookstore in a bit?"

"Yeah, okay," I said, blinking for the first time in an hour. "I'm almost done with this level."

"Okay. Well, the game'll be over in twenty minutes; we'll go then."

About an hour later, after the hockey game really ended and I died, started over, and died again more times than I would care to admit, we hopped in the truck and drove to the Borders bookstore at the mall. Once inside, I ignored what Dad was doing. The sections he was looking in were full of books that were over my head, things I didn't expect to be reading for years. Small print? Hundreds of pages? I'd take a quick Goosebumps any day, thank you very much. It was a disservice I did myself that I have long since come to regret. Dad was always bugging me to read Tolkien, and Mom tried and failed to jump-start my interest in comics one birthday with the *Death of Superman* trade paperback. I'm man enough now to admit that I should have been reading *The Hobbit* and comic books instead of R. L. Stine. I eventually came around, but on that particular afternoon I was browsing the young readers' section for *Are You There, Cthulhu? It's Me, Margaret*, or *Marrow-Sucking Lunch Ladies from Planet Death*, or whatever the latest Goosebumps yarn was when Dad found me and told me he was done and ready to go. In the truck he handed me his books.

"Take a look." Dad sounded excited, eager for me to see the surprise purchases he had made. "Call me crazy, but I think you're going to like today's haul."

From what I assumed was a bag full of Tom Clancy books or maybe a new stack of biographies on Stonewall Jackson, I pulled out two Star Wars paperbacks written by Timothy Zahn, the first two volumes of his Thrawn trilogy.

"No way!"

"Pretty cool, huh? It's not a new movie, but it's better than nothing, right?"

The books were set five years after the events of *Return of the Jedi*, and they set the tone for the Star Wars canon that followed over the course of the next decade—Han and Leia were married and expecting children, Luke was a Jedi Master, and a New Republic had formed from the ashes and hopes of the Galactic Civil War.

The name Zahn was not new to me. Neither was a new Star Wars trilogy. A few months earlier I had overheard what I thought to be nothing more than wishful thinking from the older kids at school. Now my Dad was filling my head with these same half-truths and wondrous rumors of new Star Wars movies. I hung on his every word.

"Supposedly, they're working on them now," Dad said, "and these books are the trilogy that happens after *Return of the Jedi*."

My head spun at the idea of expanding upon the saga's past and future. It all made sense. The movies were numbered four, five, and six, something that alluded to an assumed past but never to a certain future. I saw the Roman numerals in my head—I, II, III, and VII, VIII, IX. Six new Star Wars movies.

"Who knows," Dad hypothesized while I melted into the passenger seat, "maybe they'll make these books into movies after they film the trilogy that happens before the old one."

I quit Goosebumps cold turkey.

By sixth grade my knowledge of the galaxy far, far away was not to be questioned. After Dad knocked the first domino down with the Thrawn trilogy, we both jumped headfirst into the Expanded Universe. I tore through as many of the novels as Dad would buy. My favorite was Kevin J. Anderson's *Dark Apprentice*, part two of the Jedi Academy trilogy. Dad was happy enough with the novels, but I had developed an insatiable lust for any and all of the ancillary material that was associated with the Star Wars brand. At lunch and on weekends, David and I would pore over his copy of *A Guide to the Star Wars Universe* and the *Dark Empire* comics, which chronicled the resurrection of the Emperor and Luke's dangerous flirtation with the dark side. Computer games like *X-Wing* and *TIE Fighter* trumped homework and for the first time in years my room was seeing a steady influx of new action figures.

All of this was a healthy, if mildly obsessive, childhood fascination, but then there was the Star Wars Customizable Card Game, quite possibly one of the most psychotic obsessions my parents ever had to deal with. It turned its players into addicts. David, Jason, and I would spend countless hours flipping through stacks of cards, formulating strategies, brokering deals, and daydreaming about the cards sure to come out in future expansion sets. Mackie, a new kindred spirit, was also knee-deep in those small pieces of cardboard that devoured all of our allowances faster than we could earn them.

"I didn't know you played Star Wars," I said to Mackie after noticing a couple of loose cards on his kitchen table.

"Play it?" Mackie ran upstairs and came back down with a giant Tupperware container and dumped his massive collection at my feet. "I live it!"

Every waking thought was dedicated to that game. Lunch, recess, you name it; when the cards were out, we were left alone, because suddenly it was as if we were speaking some strange, impenetrable language.

"I got a cool new Lost Interrupt," Mackie would report.

"Oh yeah, what's its deploy?" David would ask.

"Two Force, one if it's for a smuggler or scoundrel. Adds plus-one to destiny draws less than three unless a lightsaber's in play, in which case it's minus one."

"Unless you're using it on a tauntaun, right?" Jason chimed in.

"Oh yeah, I think I've heard of this," I said.

"No, you're right, I'm sorry," Mackie corrected himself. "Plus-one on a smuggler, lightsaber penalty nullified, supposing you're using it on a tauntaun."

Not even weekly trips to Bradford Ski Resort—which was really just a big hill with chair lifts that was twenty minutes from school, nowhere near any mountains and nothing like a resort—could distract us from deployment costs, destiny draws, and the probability of ever getting Darth Vader in a booster pack.

"It'll never happen," Jason said, despite his unparalleled fortune in getting a Leia Organa card in his very first pack.

"He's too rare. And worth like over sixty bucks. None of us are ever going to get one."

"He's not too rare if you buy enough cards, right?" I theorized.

"I don't think that makes sense. . . ."

It got to the point where I was actually dreaming about certain cards. This was a level of obsession that even my fellow addicts had a hard time handling.

"I dreamt I got Obi-Wan in a booster last night," I confessed to David one day at recess while we stomped relish packets to see how far we could squirt them.

"I think you have a problem, man." Stomp! Splat! "Seriously, you might want to think about laying off the cards, or at least quit buying them for a little while."

Time spent deliberating, trading, and speculating over the cards we had and wished we'd get far outweighed any amount of time we spent playing the game. We didn't fully grasp the rules. In fact, they were so confusing that we didn't even know that we didn't know how to play. We were so ignorant to that fact that David and I thought it would be a great idea to try our luck at a regional Star Wars card game tournament.

The contestants were a herd of nerd stereotypes, ranging from too skinny to too fat, from balding to sporting ponytails. Acne glistened through patchy, cheese-doodle-crusted beards, and the one guy in the tie-dyed shirt with Chewbacca's snarling mug on the front was hard to take seriously, even for a twelve-year-old. It was one of two tournaments we made our parents take us to, and though Dad was "happy" to drive us to that first one, he vowed never to do anything like it again.

It was one of those instances when, despite his being a closet nerd, Dad's guy factor really kicked in. When he walked us into the tournament to sign up and make sure we were all set, I could see the look in his eyes, a look that said, "So *this* is what I've spawned." As he took in the sight of a couple dozen pock-marked, balding Peter Pans, he saw my future: at the age of thirty I would still be living at home, my teeth yellowed from a diet consisting solely of Cool Ranch Doritos, Pop Rocks, and brown sugar spooned straight out of a five-pound bag. In this terrifying "What if?" scenario, I have a bad case of tennis elbow from excessive computer gaming and chronic masturbation. Given that I have no job and no friends, he has long given up on the hope that I will set foot outside again, save for trips to the store for more junk food and blank tapes on which to record episodes of *Mystery Science Theater 3000*. (Technological advancements have shown that this would not necessarily be true. Dad's waking nightmare lacked the foresight to consider such Promethean bestowments as Netflix and TiVo, which would eliminate any real need for his giant nerd son to ever have to leave the vacuum-sealed confines of his nerd sanctuary.)

After shaking himself loose from the clutches of horror-fueled delirium, he got out of there as quickly as he could. It must have taken every ounce of energy he could muster to suppress the urge to distribute wedgies, swirlies, and demands for lunch money equally among the crowd, no nerd left behind. But he did okay. He bit his tongue, gripped his Tom Clancy book tight enough to rip it in two, and told us he'd be in the truck for the next few hours, reading.

"If you need anything, come get me," he told us. "If I'm not there, I just went to Dunkin's, and I'll only be a minute."

What he meant was, "I'll be outside trying to figure out the best way I can run myself over with my own car, and if one of these geeks so much as looks at me, I'm going to beat him so bad he won't be able to tell a Wookiee from an Ewok. If I'm not there, it's because I decided to abandon you and I won't be coming back, ever."

I can only imagine how he would have tweaked if the gamers had caught him reading one of our Star Wars books that day. Could he have kept his cool while some fanboy went on and on about the Solo children or the hotness of Mara Jade, Luke's Jedi wife?

During the tournament David and I got, to put it mildly, the shit beaten out of us. We were the youngest players there by at least ten years, greener than grass, and everyone knew it. For the most part the players were as relentless as they were nerdy. It certainly didn't help that we didn't know how to play correctly. One guy noticed that I clearly didn't know what I was doing right from the get-go.

"Whoa. Whoa whoa whoa. Kid." The tone in his voice was something between annoyed and depressed. "What the hell are you doing?"

"I'm deploying a medical droid," I explained.

"Why?"

"It's all I got."

The guy let out a slow, painful sigh. It was the depression equivalent of the mythical brown note. I was instantly bummed out.

"Give me the cards in your hand, man," he demanded.

"Isn't that cheating?"

"You were going to lose anyway, right?"

"No?"

"Give me the cards. I'm going to show you how this works. Shit, at least one of us will get something out of this."

My irritated instructor spent the better part of the game explaining to me exactly how he was beating me so bad. By the end of the day I had only won one game, and it was against the guy who propped his good-luck IG-88 action figure on the table next to his stacks of cards. It would seem that his mechanical soldier of fortune wasn't smiling down on him that day if a kid who couldn't even wrap his head around the rules of the game managed to beat him. But who am I to talk? My black magic wasn't working either; my lucky Boba Fett T-shirt was leaving me just as high and dry.

David came out of it all slightly less defeated than I did, with two or three wins. His stand-out victory was over a guy who insisted upon deploying a Blizzard Walker—one of three he was allowed to have in play at any given time—at Death Star Hangar 324, where it served no discernable purpose.

"It was stupid!" David raged during the lunch break.

"What are you supposed to do with it there?" I asked, hot-dog chunks flying out of my mouth to illustrate just how confused I was by such a lame move.

"I know! He said it was for Presence, but come on! It was so stupid!"

I just want to state for all but the two of you out there who have no idea what any of that exchange meant, that I have no idea what that exchange meant. I couldn't even begin to explain why it irritated us so much. It just mattered. Trust me.

The time in between games—which we had a lot of since we were getting beaten so often and so quickly—was spent browsing the booths that the attending vendors had set up.

Owners of hobby and comic shops from several nearby towns had booster packs and starter decks for sale, all of which we happily indulged in. They also had awesome individual cards at awesomely unreasonable prices! We'd drool over Obi-Wan Kenobi and Yoda cards because we knew we'd never get one. For the price of one of these rare cards you could almost buy a whole box of booster packs from a wholesaler, something David and I squandered all our Christmas money on two years in a row. This got us a few good cards, but never the ones we saw behind a pane of glass with orange, $60 price tags slapped on their slipcases. Still, we'd look and drool, thinking about how badass our deck would be if only we had that one killer card.

"Getting that Vader card is all I need for an unstoppable dark side deck," I confessed to David.

"You wish," he responded as he flipped through the Dagobah pack he'd just bought. "These guys have at least three Vaders in their decks, not to mention any number of other awesome cards that we don't have. Come on, the next game's about to start."

Not a day went by that year when we didn't have our cards on hand. Even if we didn't play or trade, we'd want to have them with us. Cards were meticulously filed and organized by expansion set and by side and type. I kept super-rare cards, like main characters, their personal weapons, and, while I had it, the *Millennium Falcon*, in a three-ring binder. Between the four of us who played—David, Jason, Mackie, and me—no one got a pack of cards without letting the others know about it.

We were like little girls, lying belly down on our beds, twirling the phone cord in our fingers and giggling over whatever awesome, rare new card we'd just gotten in a pack.

"Dude, I just got Son of Skywalker in a Dagobah pack!" Jason swooned over the phone.

"Son of Skywalker? I read in *Tiger Beat* that he's immune to attrition less than four and once per game you can deploy a lightsaber on him for free!" Giggle, giggle.

"(Sigh) . . . Isn't he just dreamy?"

More important than any dollar value that some card-gaming magazine would arbitrarily assign to our rare cards or any game we ever won was the history the cards told. Each card contained a bit of Star Wars lore specific to the image printed on its face. We learned of home worlds, back stories, and the merchants of war who built the Rebel and Imperial fleets. No one soaked up that information quite like Mackie. To this day, he can rattle off a short bio of even the most seemingly insignificant Rebel soldier stationed at Echo Base and will challenge anyone to ask him an obscure question.

"Okay. What's the number for the trash compactor Luke was stuck in?" some cocky nonfanatic might ask, thinking they've stumped the all-knowing Mackie.

"Three-two-six-three-eight-two-seven. Please," he'd answer without batting an eyelash, "don't insult me. Ask me a hard one."

"What do you mean, 'Ask me a hard one'? That was a hard one."

"Oh come on, ask me something about Zev Senesca."

"Who the hell is Zev Senesca?"

Our discussions would go on for hours as we dissected the most obscure bit of Star Wars trivia. Over time my brain has atrophied and I have forgotten a lot of what I once knew, but

I can still tell you a few things. For example, Sienar Fleet Systems manufactured TIE fighters, Han's blaster was a modified BlasTech DL-44, and before *Episode II* came and solidified what was then just speculative history, it was generally understood that Luke's uncle, Owen Lars, was in fact Obi-Wan Kenobi's brother. Cool as that might have been, it's not exactly the kind of opening line chicks go for. Obi-Wan and Owen were bros + cute girl at the bar = you naked with nothing but ice cream and comics to keep you company.

CHAPTER 8

SOMETHING SPECIAL

THE YEAR 1997 BROUGHT WITH it a dream come true for my generation of Star Wars fans, something the trailers for the special edition re-release made sure to point out. We were an entire population of fandom who had only seen Star Wars on TV sets, the previews reminded us, and therefore we hadn't really seen Star Wars at all. Truer words had never been spoken. We knew the movies inside and out. We could recite them in our sleep, but to see them in all their twenty-by-forty-foot glory, that was going to be something else entirely. We were about to receive the gift of practically seeing them for the first time all over again. I was bouncing off the walls. In all my life up to that point, I had never bounced off anything. On the spectrum of other kids' opinions, Star Wars landed somewhere between "gay" and "retarded" and would stay that way until Super Bowl XXXI aired a Pepsi commercial where Darth

Vader—up on the big screen—crushed a kid's soda cup because he was slurping too loudly.

"We're going this weekend, right?" I asked, while my dad fought off the urge to weep as the Patriots lost the big game. "Dad?"

"Yeah. Sure. What difference does it make?" It wasn't even halftime and his voice dripped with defeat.

I looked back to the TV and zoned out, wishing for that commercial to be replayed.

"Sweet."

The next day at school it was one of the more-talked-about Super Bowl commercials. No one wanted to talk about the game, that's for sure—not after the trouncing our New England Patriots had gotten from those cheese-eating bastards from Green Bay. The hallway musings over that "cool *Star Wars* Pepsi commercial" were my first run-ins with the deep-seated hypocrisy within every kid who ever called Star Wars lame.

Star Wars: Episode IV—A New Hope, as the re-release of *Star Wars* was now officially going by, opened the weekend after the Super Bowl and it was a Pacitti family event. On a gray Saturday morning, neither so bright nor so early, we waited in a short line for the day's first showing at the Salisbury Cinema 6. A few feet behind us was a redheaded kid a year or so younger than me dressed up as Han Solo. Mom thought it was a riot, but I was just annoyed.

"Look at that kid!" Mom said, nudging me to turn and look.

"Yup," I said with a grunt. Because of my own insecurities, my younger self always had a problem with people who dress up as fictional characters for occasions other than Halloween or costume parties. I just assumed that if I ever tried to pull off something like going out in public dressed as Han Solo, I'd get my ass kicked. I lightened up as I got older, and it became fun to see a group of fans dressed as stormtroopers with bulging waistlines, or a Fellowship of the Ring that was short one Pippin but had an extra Samwise. But on that particular February morning, I was just hoping that Lil' Han was going to sit quietly during the movie. His getup was enough to prove just how much he loved Star Wars; I didn't need him shouting out, "I have a bad feeling about this!" or "Let the Wookiee win!" during the show.

As each installment of the trilogy came and went in the theaters over the course of the next few months, Star Wars momentum picked up at a ridiculous pace. Soon every walk of sixth-grade life was infected with the pop-culture bug that was Star Wars. It was on fast-food bags, the toys were back in a big way, and every kid had a favorite character and scene. It was, from what my parents have told me, like 1977 all over again. And I hated it. This exclusive little club, this refuge from all the guff I had ever been given in the time between when I got on and off the school bus had just opened its doors to the rest of the world.

I distinctly remember one popular girl gushing to the point of nearly fainting about what a stud Han Solo was.

"He's so cute!" she squealed. I struggled to keep my mouth shut while I imagined her room, walls painted pink and plastered in posters of dreamy turds like Jonathan Taylor Thomas or the brothers from Hanson. David and I were in the thick of an important card trade as she passed by.

"Ohmygod! Is that a Han Solo card?" she asked. "Can I see it?"

I flipped the card's face to her but kept it just out of reach. No way in hell was I about to let some bandwagoner, a girl no less, get her mitts on my rare Cloud City iteration of Han Solo.

"Come on. Can I hold it, please?"

No you can't. You make me sick. I don't want you or your stink anywhere near my cards.

"Um, well, actually, I'd rather you didn't," I squeaked. "It's sort of valuable." *Yeah, man, stick it to her!*

Suddenly the popular girls were swooning over the dashing Han Solo, and guys with their hormones about to go supernova were drooling over Princess Leia's metal slave bikini like it was something new. It wasn't! I'd been drooling over it for years! This was my galaxy, damn it, and I didn't want the cool kids to have any fun in it. They had hogged everything else, and now they were peeking into my little world? No, they weren't just peeking, they were staking their claims and suddenly they all thought they were experts on the galaxy I had spent countless hours ensconcing myself in.

My disappearing claim on Star Wars dwindled during an oral book report on the novelization of *A New Hope.* My presentation was going to be sublime. Using Star Wars cards and the movies as references, I drew an awesome poster of Vader's Star Destroyer chasing Leia's blockade runner over Tatooine. I typed up my report to look like the movie's intro text scroll and stapled it over black construction paper to look like a patch of empty, black space. It was, to date, the zenith of my artistic career. Surely if George Lucas ever saw it, saw the loving/borderline-psychotic attention to detail, he would instantly give me a job at Industrial Light & Magic as a concept artist. I'd have skipped high school and college, moved out to San Francisco, and become the special-effects industry's equivalent of Doogie Howser.

After giving a rousing five-minute summary and film-to-book comparison, I opened the floor to questions, not expecting any of my classmates to raise their hand, because no one ever did, and was shocked when a girl's hand went up.

"Your poster's wrong," she said matter-of-factly.

I spun on my heels and looked at the poster clipped to the blackboard behind me. Nothing was missing. Everything was drawn to scale and the perspective was accurate. Every color and laser burn was exactly on point. The girl was a total quack.

"No, it isn't," I said, dismissing her comment as some feeble attempt by a Star Wars neophyte to sound like she knew what was up when she undeniably did not.

"Yeah, it is. Isn't Darth Vader's ship supposed to be round?"

For a second the question tripped me up. *She couldn't mean the Death Star*, I thought. *It's not even a ship.* Either way, I decided to indulge her. "No, you're thinking of the Death Star. That's something else. This is the Star Destroyer that he was chasing Princess Leia in."

I went to take my seat, but she wouldn't let up.

"No, it's wrong!" she argued. "His ship is round!"

"No! You're thinking of something else!"

David piped in and tried to talk her down. "He's right, this is the—"

"Why won't you just admit that it's wrong?" she cut him off, determined to undermine my authority.

"Seriously?" I demanded. "You don't think I know what I'm talking about?"

I fantasized about grabbing her by the ponytail and shaking the life out of her.

"Look at me!" I'd yell, spraying spit and chewed-up bits of hot lunch in her face. "I have a Boba-fucking-Fett T-shirt on and I've been forced to keep my love for this movie a secret until all of the sudden you assholes realized that, yes, it is actually the greatest movie in the world! I know the difference between a Star Destroyer and the Death Star! You don't think I do? Who do you think you are to tell me I don't?!"

While I stood at the front of the room, fists shaking, eye twitching, and Satan stoking the fires of hate in my gut, our teacher stepped up, thanked me for my wonderful presentation, and asked me to kindly take my seat. I sat, but I didn't like it. Mad that I didn't get to win the debate and get a standing ovation from the only two other nerds in the class, I seethed through the rest of the afternoon. And the rest of the year. Obviously I'm still seething about it. In fact, I want it on my tombstone: "Here lies Tony Pacitti. If nothing else, he knew more about Star Wars than some stupid girl who only started liking it way after he did."

While these bandwagon Jedi and fair-weather fanboys rained further destruction on my already flimsy faith in the integrity of my fellow man, a glimmer of hope came from the most unlikely of sources. I could now actually sort of pretend to ignore the assholes who prowled my neighborhood. My skin had, through necessity, grown thicker. Their barbs still cut deep, but at least I was making it harder for them to be able to tell that.

Every kid in the neighborhood from age seven to eleven was calling me Nolan now, picking on me exclusively because Queef had moved on to junior high, and I was the only poor dweeb left at the bus stop. It was old hat. It was boring, and I was sick of fighting back, so with my head down I'd sneak in a few rounds of *Tetris* for Game Boy on the bus under their jeers, or maybe bring a Walkman and let the Presidents of the United States of America drown out their attacks with "Lump" and "Peaches." I just didn't care anymore. I had friends now. Just a few, but friends nonetheless, so what did a couple of short, irritating bus rides a day really matter in the long run? I had also become quite skillful in the art of deluding myself.

One day in class I had excused myself to use the bathroom, a clever trick I had learned in the wake of peeing my pants and telling everybody about it. When I walked in, Kevin, one of the neighborhood guys, was taking a leak. I sighed, rolled my eyes, and hoped that whatever asshole thing he had to say he'd just say it already and be on his way. I unzipped and started my business. He flushed, zipped up, and washed his hands. Silence. Not a goddamned peep. I watched out of the corner of my eye as he left. When he reached for the door, he stopped, turned halfway around, and looked at me for a minute.

"Hey," he said, "do you like it when we call you Nolan?"

"No," I replied with a calm confidence that I had probably contracted by coming into contact with something in the bathroom that a more self-assured kid had sneezed on. "No, I don't like it at all."

Kevin paused, then nodded. "Okay," he said. "I won't do it anymore," and he walked out of the bathroom.

The rest of the guys followed Kevin's lead, or his orders— I'm not sure which. It doesn't matter which. By springtime, the boys whom I had once regarded as the bane of my crummy prepubescent existence were my friends.

Seriously, could it be that I finally had friends whose houses I could walk to? Another small handful of people I wouldn't be afraid to bump into in the hallway or talk to on the bus? It was weird, but suddenly I was no longer the low man on the totem pole. I had stumbled into an alternate reality where I was standing on my own two feet, speaking to kids I never would have made eye contact with before, and Star Wars was the hottest thing on the globe again.

At first I was too willing to jump to the conclusion that everyone was a filthy, lying hypocrite, but I soon came up with a new theory. Hypocrisy wasn't the name of the game. They—we—were all growing up. The "cool" kids started to talk to me not just because I had started to come out of my shell by way of the double-edged sword of Star Wars' popularity. They finally saw that I wasn't a bad kid. Hell, I was even kind of funny. Kevin didn't even need to see that side of me; he just genuinely felt bad for how they had treated me, and in a very grown-up move for a twelve-year-old, manned up and apologized.

I started talking to those guys on the bus, at lunch, and between classes, and I began to see that they weren't all that bad themselves. It dawned on me that maybe I wasn't exactly uncool—maybe I was just shy. Somewhere underneath all that frustration and schoolyard misery was an all-right kid who just needed that right moment to poke his head out. I had gotten off to a rocky start in Rowley, and of all things it was Star Wars, the very thing that served as my security blanket, that became the common ground I shared with my classmates for those last months of elementary school.

I was filled with a strange, tingly feeling. It was warm and encouraging, and years down the road I would be able to pinpoint it. It was optimism. Weird, right? Suddenly I found myself walking through the hallways much easier. The everpresent specter of an unwarranted insult, shove, or reminder of that time all those years ago when I wet my pants had just disappeared. I soaked in the moment. *So this is what it feels like not to be waiting for another bottom to drop out.*

Just as things suddenly seemed to be changing for me, Star Wars was going through some rather monumental personality shifts as well. Thanks to the special-effects breakthroughs made with *Jurassic Park*, Lucas had decided that it was finally time to make the trilogy the way he had always envisioned it. This meant adding things, changing things, and becoming something different from what I had come to know so intimately. At the time it didn't matter all that much to me. It was still *Star Wars* on the big screen. I was happier than I could possibly describe.

A New Hope had been given a shiny new skin. New, digital men, women, and monsters suddenly populated the background of Mos Eisley in an effort to give the impression that people actually did live in this fictional world. *Empire* was given a similar treatment in terms of flashier visuals and a greater sense of there being an actual hustling and bustling population at the Cloud City. We also got Greedo shooting first, something Lucas justified by saying that Han was a good guy and should have been forced to kill Greedo. He didn't want Han to be a bad role model for a new generation, despite twenty years of his being a smuggler, scoundrel, and criminal who was eventually redeemed through his role in the Rebellion. My uncle had grown up worshipping the version where Han shot first. Now he's a cop. Go figure.

But when *The Return of the Jedi* rolled around that March, I found myself questioning, for the first time, the infallible vision of George. It was released in theaters just a week or so before my twelfth birthday, and Mom took me, David, Jason, and Mackie to see it. Things were sailing smoothly at first, with a sharper picture, better sound, and a few new effects here and there, but a digitally enhanced Max Rebo Band made me do a double-take.

What had previously filled the great hall of Jabba's palace—a weird sort of space jazz—had been replaced with flat-out Jake and Elwood blues. As the band finished up its first tune, a very computer-generated cross between James Brown and the Honeycombs cereal mascot began counting off to a frog playing a sci-fi harmonica. When they settled on a key, the band's horn section blasted the opening chord of a new song, "Jedi Rocks," and lead singer Sy Snootles, reanimated in full, CGI glory, came off as more Muppety then ever. In fact, between her pouting lips breaking the fourth wall, her tacky-looking backup singers, and the Honeycomb guy, I'd have preferred if George had just asked Jim Henson's kids if he could borrow Dr. Teeth and the Electric Mayhem from *The Muppet Show.*

As exciting as seeing *Return of the Jedi* in the theater was, the experience left a bit of a funny taste in my mouth along with the stale movie-theater popcorn. The popcorn taste was easy enough to get rid of, but no amount of toothpaste and elbow grease could scrub out the taste that *Jedi* left behind. *Jedi* was bumped, officially, down two slots, thus beginning my short stint of saying, "Not that it means I really like any one less than another, but I like them all in order from first to last."

I could never confess my fears, at least not yet. It felt like a betrayal. I was upset enough by what I was feeling, but imagine what would have happened if I told someone:

"Guys, I'm not so sure about what just happened in *Jedi*. I mean, did we really need a giant clam to come up out of the Sarlacc?"

"What are you saying?" Mackie would ask, his face unable to hide the feeling that he had just been stabbed in the back.

"No, nothing, I just mean, was that louder, flashier music scene really necessary?"

"I'd appreciate it if you gave me all of your Star Wars cards and never spoke to any of us again."

What all these changes, even the most minor and inoffensive ones, failed to do was add to my overall experience of the movies. Never has there been a better argument for the old adage "If it ain't broke, don't fix it." It didn't take long for me to start to question the changes. Why? Why bother? I would have been perfectly happy to see exactly what I had on tape at home play out on the big screen. It wasn't about not liking Star Wars; it was about not liking what was happening to it. I was finally learning that what mattered was being true to one's self, not trying to be something you aren't. Star Wars, in 1997, struck me as being insecure about itself. It's like Lucas thought he had to keep up with the Joneses by throwing in all those new, top-of-the-line effects. But we aren't talking about some long-forgotten, rinky-dink sci-fi flick from the 1960s. This was fucking Star Wars, the granddaddy of the modern-day special-effects-driven blockbuster.

After the movie, Mom drove us to the comic book store for some post-*Jedi* card-buying action. The rest of the day was spent wheeling and dealing with our dark and light side decks, basking in the greatness of what were then cutting-edge special effects and what, as far as we were concerned, was the greatest story ever told. I kept my concerns to myself because at the end of that particular day the only thing that mattered was that we had done it. We had finally seen Star Wars the way our parents had always said it should be seen. Even better was that their re-release was not just a celebration of the original's twentieth anniversary, but a confirmation that *Episode I*, *II*, and *III* were not the stuff of legend but the stuff of science-fiction fact. A new trilogy, an actual Star Wars my generation could call its own, loomed on the horizon like Tatooine's binary suns.

EPISODE II

COOL AS TATOOINE

CHAPTER 9

JUNIOR HIGH: WHERE CHILDHOOD GOES TO DIE

IT WAS A HOT, BORING day in August. I was cleaning out the garage as Dad had requested, when the phone rang. I answered the ancient rotary-dial phone we had hanging on the wall next to the even-more-ancient Frigidaire we kept out there for things like beer and extra gallons of milk. A classmate, Justin, was on the other end, and while I dribbled a basketball around the spot where Mom usually parked her van we shot the shit about what we were going to do with ourselves once seventh grade—junior high—started in a couple of weeks.

"What kind of jeans you gonna get?" he asked.

"Blue ones," I said, missing the point of the question and writing it off as a joke.

"Make sure you get baggy ones, man. Everyone's going to be wearing them baggy. I got a couple of pairs of JNCOs the other day."

I didn't know what the hell a JNCO was. I'd come to find out they were pretty ridiculous, but at the time they were a white-hot trend I wouldn't be in on. Justin, on the other hand, wouldn't be left out of the loop. Justin was one of those kids, one of those social everymen, who seemed to have friends in all strata of the schoolyard pecking order. He was also loud, very loud, and hysterical to boot. He was the guy who, during in-class tryouts for the sixth-grade spelling bee the previous school year, decided he was done and took a dive in the second round.

"Okay Justin, the word is *Petunia*."

"Petunia," he repeated with the textbook definition of a shit-eating grin. "Petunia. P-E-T ... uh ... Unia! Petunia!" And with hands raised to hush the cheers and laughs, he took his seat with all the playful arrogance any self-respecting class clown should have.

I never gave much thought to my wardrobe, because my mother still had a kung fu grip on final say when it came to what I could and couldn't leave the house wearing. So I wrote off his well-meaning heads-up and had one less fight with my mom when we went out to buy new clothes for school. But he was right. Good lord, was Justin right about those damned jeans.

The first day of seventh grade revealed that an over-whelming majority of the pants at Triton Regional Junior High School were in fact JNCO. Pairs of these big, floppy denim curtains hung off almost every guy and a whole bunch of the girls, each adorned with some goofy-looking graffiti-styled cartoon character sewn onto one of the back pockets. And then there was me, standing there with my ultraconservative Lee blue jeans that fit the way pants were meant to, hating every minute of it. I also lacked a different 2Pac or

Biggie memorial T-shirt for every day of the week, but since I had no idea who 2Pac or Biggie were, I didn't feel as bad about that one.

Any hang-ups spawned by my own fashion faux pas were briefly put on the back burner once I managed to get a look at what was going on in the higher altitudes of my female peers' anatomy. There we were, in the spring of our young lives, and all of the lovely young ladies were starting to bud and blossom.

Boobs. Were. Everywhere.

From every angle I was being assaulted by perky preteen breasts, taunting me with their siren songs in the keys of A and B cup. Some girls were just starting to sprout, while a few more rapidly developing wet dreams incarnate were already wielding their breasts like a Jedi wields the Force and its strong influence over the weak-minded. The line had been drawn in the sand. The girls were becoming women, and we boys were becoming the drooling apes of men we were destined to be.

Junior high made me the low man on the totem pole all over again. My revelation the year before that maybe we were all going to start to get along had no bearing here. Junior high was a wasteland of clashing egos, overstimulated hormones, and fractured self-esteem. I had thought kids were cruel before, but seventh and eighth grade were eye openers. Those years were relentless, and I didn't even get the brunt of it. Kids whose faces looked like acne-riddled combat zones or who had unfortunate cases of overbearing B.O. were torn apart by the cackling, heartless bastards they were forced to call their peers. For the most part I was left alone, so I watched, terrified, and waited for the vultures to hone in on me and pick my corpse clean.

I may have been right about the kids from Rowley attaining some level of civility with one another. We had grown up together and learned each other's personalities: which buttons to press, which ones not to. Even if you weren't really someone's friend, at least you knew the kid's name. But in my junior high, with a whole slew of unknowns dumped into the equation from the towns of Newbury and Salisbury, the variables had changed. I was now one of a class of about 300. I didn't matter. I was nothing. I was just a flounder among sharks.

Or was I? There was only one time in the two years of junior high that I can actually remember being bullied at school. Some kid whose name and face I can't even recall was standing in front of my locker. I asked him to move and, like the asshole he was, he asked what I was going to do about it. I figured that junior high was like prison, and if I showed that I was hard early on, then no one would try to stab me or rape me in the lunch line.

"Hey, can you move, please?" I asked.

He responded with a super-douchey, "What are you going to do about it if I don't?"

Being infinitely clumsy, I didn't even lay a hand on him. He took a step back when I tried to push him away, and I fell flat on my face while he stood over me, laughing with his friend. I was mortified. It was the second day of school and I was convinced that this was what the rest of the year was going to be like. I didn't even want to get up. I just lay there, kissing tile, hoping that maybe someone would stomp on the back of my head and put me out of my misery.

"Hey!" I heard a new voice yell from above, where all the normal kids were busy with their between-class routines. There was a quick shuffle of feet and what sounded like a body getting tossed against a locker. Nervously, I looked up. Chris, the same Chris who had beaten me up at the bus stop all those years ago, had the guy by the shirt and was getting up in his face.

"Leave him the fuck alone! Okay?"

"Yeah, man, I was just messin' around with him."

Chris let him go and instantly switched out of attack mode.

"Cool. Thanks man," he said, smiling, then proceeded to talk with the guy as if nothing had happened. After he walked away, Chris held out a hand and helped me to my feet.

"You okay, Nolan?" he asked.

"Yeah, I guess." The bell rang and we went our separate ways.

That was the extent of my physical torment. If that was what trying to get something out of my locker was going to be like, then what other horrors would those hallways contain? It was enough to push me into a sort of self-imposed emotional and conversational exile from the rest of my classmates, despite the fact that I was perfectly situated, socially speaking, in the middle of the road. I was vanilla at my worst, cheese pizza at my most extroverted.

Clearly there were kids higher up in the schoolyard pecking order who had my back. I had spent the summer before seventh grade getting reacquainted with the guys in the neighborhood, who were now friends instead of bullies or douchebags to avoid at all costs. In the wake of Kevin's apology, Nolan had become an affectionate nickname, with my acceptance of it standing as a testament to my surprising ability to forgive the guys for all the shit they had given me. Chris and his brother Joey had rented a copy of *GoldenEye 007* for Nintendo 64, so most days were spent at their place, shooting up the Facility and debating whether or not Oddjob should be declared illegal to use.

"He's only like two feet tall!" Queef complained after suffering repeated losses at Oddjob's diminutive hands. "He's too hard to kill. I say he's off limits."

"You only say he's off limits when you can't play him, Queef," said Joey. This was followed by a rocket blast and the Bond-themed "you just died" jingle.

The game was several weeks overdue, but until they were able to buy a copy to own, we all pitched in for the late fees. The brotherhood of proximity that I had once feared was now a brotherhood of genuine interest.

Junior high featured plenty of kids who were most certainly worse off than I. If you were to look at me back then, there was nothing to instantly label me as an easy target. I didn't wear the cool clothes, but my wardrobe wasn't about to invite any unwanted attention. I had a bit of an acne problem, but not as bad as some. I didn't have braces, and I no longer needed glasses. I was perfectly invisible to the kinds of kids who looked for someone to dump on. Strangely enough, it may have been that invisibility that was the problem. At least when I was picked on, there was a reason for my misery. Now there was no feedback coming my way, no one to tell me what I was doing wrong. I told myself I was dirt and figured that as long as I tried to keep a low profile, no one would waste the time to tell me I was right in thinking that I sucked.

By the end of the first week of school I was back in my shell, undoing those itsy-bitsy baby steps forward I had taken the year before. As if being extremely shy to begin with wasn't enough, there was no longer any common ground for me to find with all these new faces. I was conversationally outgunned by kids who had spent every day of the summer watching MTV, a teenage institution that my parents still declared forbidden fruit. My finger was so far from the pulse of anything remotely cool that trying to keep up would be suicide. I had been living under a rock. Star Wars on the big screen felt like a lifetime ago. Now all anyone could talk about and imitate to death was Austin Powers. What the fuck was an Austin Powers? Who the hell was Carson Daly?

I was so confused, in over my head, and completely paranoid about what others thought about me that when my mother came home one day with Star Wars bed sheets for me, I broke down and cried. I begged her to take them back.

"Please," I pleaded, "just take them back!"

"But Tone—"

"What if someone sees them? Then what?"

My mother looked at me as if I were a stranger. She didn't know where this sudden rejection of Star Wars was coming from. All she could offer was a cold, detached, "If you say so."

She returned the sheets and I never saw them again. Never got a chance to take them out of their plastic wrap, bundle myself inside them, and tell them how sorry I was for being ashamed of them. I can't imagine who I thought would have set foot in my room who was in any sort of position to take me down a peg for having Star Wars sheets. It was in these dark days so soon after Star Wars had became a giant again that things started to feel like they were getting away from me. Junior high was too much for me to handle, and for the first time since I was seven years old, George Lucas's world was unable to provide sanctuary.

Nothing felt the same. What I'd thought were basic principles or universal truths had been proven wrong. Junior high was Bizarro World, the Mirror Universe, and *Planet of the Apes* all rolled into one tragically awkward, two-year-long episode of *The Twilight Zone.*

CHAPTER 10

DISTURBANCES IN THE FORCE

IF THERE WAS A BRIGHT side at all to any of this, it was that Jason and I were back in some classes together for the first time since the second grade. But even this was a bittersweet moment, a sign that nothing was safe from the corrupting sickness that my parents called growing up. Jason showed up to the first day of seventh grade wearing a Rage Against the Machine T-shirt reeking of Marlboro Lights. That summer he had discovered rock 'n' roll and the inherent coolness of smoking cigarettes, thanks in part to the kids on his street. Most of them were the kinds of kids your mother always said she didn't want you hanging around.

I began to notice that when we'd get together, the conversations became shorter and shorter. If it hadn't been for video games and Star Wars cards, we probably wouldn't have gone out of our way to hang out anymore. The more Jason hung out with those other kids, the more I felt the two of us were starting to lose touch.

In March of that school year I found out just how far Jason had wandered down his new path. I had known for some time that he had been smoking. He'd told me. I'd seen it. It didn't make a difference to me one way or the other because, despite the best efforts of health teachers and antismoking ads to make me think the contrary, cigarettes didn't turn Jason into a monster. One weekend, a couple of the guys from his neighborhood and I were at Jason's house for a marathon session of *Resident Evil 2* while his parents and older sisters were out of the house for the day. We all sat cross-legged in front of the TV, blasting zombies and mixing herbs in a futile effort to survive the hordes of pixilated living dead. There were plenty of herb jokes made, all of which went over my head, and they were what spurred Jeff to make his proposal.

"You guys want to smoke a bowl?"

I knew that he meant smoke pot, but the term *bowl* was entirely foreign to me. I had this mental image of the three of them all standing over a cereal bowl with a little bonfire of marijuana burning inside of it, noses and mouths sucking at a column of yellow smoke that was curling its way up into the air.

"Pacitti, you in?" Jeff asked. Jeff, with his Dopey ears, reddish hair, and freckle-covered cheeks, was a juvenile delinquent disguised as a Norman Rockwell character, an Eddie Haskell if ever there was one.

This was my first run-in with drugs, and the fact that I thought of weed as a drug in the same sense that heroin or meth is a drug is a bit funny now. I grew up during a golden age of antidrug commercials, my favorite of which was a particularly bat-shit crazy Saturday-morning cartoon special starring a who's-who of animated characters, from Bugs Bunny to Winnie the Pooh to one of the Ninja Turtles. I couldn't help but imagine my egg of a brain frying in a pan after smoking grass with the guys. But before any of that fear could take hold, before I could even begin to think about what I had been asked or imagine what life would be like as a junkie when I grew up, I paused the game and said, "Yeah, sure, I guess."

We all stepped out into the gray afternoon. There was an inch or so of fresh late-winter powder on the back deck. My heart was racing. Jason, Jeff, Greg, and I stood around, shivering, as Jeff took the bowl, which was smaller and much less bowl-like than I had expected, out of his pocket. The bowl turned out to be no more than a bit of wood with some holes drilled into it with a piece of tinfoil resting in the larger of the holes. Jeff took out a small plastic sandwich bag with a little bit of weed left in it and packed the bowl. Jason and Greg were now visibly excited, looking like a couple of Wile E. Coyotes spying a pipe-toking Road Runner through a pair of binoculars. Me? I was panicked. Jeff took the first hit and then passed it to Jason. Greg was up next. Then it came to me.

"Put your finger over the carb—this little hole," Jeff instructed, "and when I say so, take your finger off it."

I held the bowl to my lips, blocked the hole, and waited for Jeff to fire it up.

"Inhale," he said. I started to suck in lightly. The burning weed crackled in the bowl.

"And let go of the carb."

I took my finger off, and a quick rush of smoke hit the back of my throat and went down the hatch. Jeff took the bowl and ordered me to keep it in as long as I could. When I finally exhaled, Jeff congratulated me, and the bowl started its rounds again.

"It's good, right?" he asked.

"Yeah," I coughed. "Yeah. It's good." I had no clue.

After we had killed it we went back in and picked up where we'd left off.

"Oh man," Greg groaned when the suspense that the Resident Evil franchise is so well known for started to kick in and the scares came at us in rapid succession. "Did you see those zombies, man? This game is so fucked when you're high, man, so totally fucked!"

Jason and Jeff half-cackled in agreement. Greg, on the other hand, was in stitches. Had we smoked the same weed? What had I done wrong that I was left alone, merely experiencing how regular-fucked the game was while Greg got to view it as totally fucked?

"Pacitti. Dude. How totally fucked is this game right now?"

"I don't know, Greg, uh, dude. Totally fucked, I guess?"

"Fuck me. Dude, I'm so high. . . ."

His bragging, Jason and Jeff's lack of stoner enthusiasm, and my feeling absolutely no different led me to believe that not only was Jeff's weed real garbage, but Greg was in fact as big an asshole as I thought he was for faking it.

Summertime found me at a crossroads. My best friend was heading in one direction, one where the road was paved in bowl resin and the speed limit signs were shaped like birds flipped at any form of authority. It hurt to watch him walk down it, his shape becoming harder to see through the smoke and the crowds of douchebags who kept luring him farther and farther down the road. What choice did I have but to follow him? Deep down, the friend I had always known was still there, choking for air. I told myself it would be irresponsible to let him go it alone.

Maybe I really did think—or hope—that I was some sort of lifeline. I went down Jason's street, Feldman Road, and like Luke going into the dark side cave on Dagobah, I came face-to-face with what I brought with me every time. Luke brought in his fear and his lightsaber. I brought my desperation and my bike.

Everything about the summer of '98 seemed dehydrated, choked for life and wilting, and not a single lawn was green for more than a week after the month of June had come and gone. The air was filled with stifling humidity that hung thickly, refusing to rain down and offer relief, and the world was painted in shades of orange, brown, and yellow. Memories of those days between seventh and eighth grade taste like Parliament Lights and candy stolen from Skip's Country Store, soaking with sweat, rebellion, and rock 'n' roll.

Classic rock ruled supreme during those hot summer months, with the sounds of contemporary angst and drug-fueled bacchanalia occasionally sneaking into the mix. The soundtracks of our lives were *Led Zeppelin IV*, Pink Floyd's *The Wall*, and The Doors' *Greatest Hits*, with Sublime's self-titled album and Rage Against the Machine's *Evil Empire* thrown in for good measure. We spent every one of those summer days just sitting around listening to music and chain-smoking the butts that we had acquired by dubious means. Eventually it got to the point where those few albums were played so much that they became nothing but ambient noise. They were wind blowing through the trees. Lyrics and chords blurred into the sounds of barking dogs or the crackle of somebody's cigarette. In between smokes and CDs, we'd ride our bikes from one end of Feldman Road to the other, with frequent stops in between to round up the usual suspects. Greg and Jeff were usually around, as well as a constantly rotating roster of older kids and their siblings, all faces I knew from school but never once spoke to directly or addressed by name. No one really seemed to notice my presence aside from Jason, Jeff, and Greg, who made it a point to be as much of a dick as was humanly possible.

"What're you doing here, Pacitti?" Greg would ask through a smug, snarling grin wrapped tightly around a Marlboro Red that he had lifted from his big brother.

"Hanging out, I guess."

"What? You think you're cool now, smoking cigarettes?"

"I don't do it to be cool, man."

He lit a string of fireworks and tossed them into a mailbox with the sort of nonchalance I reserved for scratching my ass. Pow! Puh-pow pow! Pow!

"Good, 'cause you're not, you homo."

That was Greg's thing. He fancied himself as some kind of tweenage badass, a kid who'd been drunk and high by the time he was twelve. One of his self-appointed claims to fame at the time was that he'd had sex with some chick who lived next door to his dad in Danvers. The fact that Danvers was twenty minutes away meant we couldn't fact-check it, couldn't shake the ol' grapevine the way we could if he'd named a girl from our school. The whole story smacked of "Yeah, I got a girlfriend. Uh . . . we met at camp. She lives in Florida. You've probably never heard of her. . . ." He was a Grade-A dick, and while Jeff could schmooze with my parents and they'd keep their real opinion of him to themselves, my folks had no qualms about telling me how much of an asshole that Greg So-and-So was. Of course, they never said asshole, but I didn't have to try too hard to read between the lines. I knew he was a scumbag.

Shit, the kid put a cigarette out in my fucking bike helmet because he thought I needed to be reminded of how gay it was that I had to wear it in the first place. "Oh come on," I whined. "What the hell'd you do that for?"

"Because I want you to remember how gay it is that you have to wear that fucking thing."

Actions speak louder than words, and anything that guy ever did was universal sign language for "I'm a huge douchebag."

This preteen rebellion was new to me. There was a language, both in body and vernacular, that I didn't understand. It wasn't unlike being in school, where I'd eavesdrop on the cool kids' conversations and could barely follow because of my limited frame of reference for then-current trends. I kept quiet, learned the code, laughed when everyone else did, and spoke up rarely, only when I felt like I had enough of a leg to stand on. I played fly on the wall to Jason's crowd, all in the hopes of maintaining our friendship when all I really wanted to do was watch *The Empire Strikes Back* and play *Crash Bandicoot* with Jason for a few hours.

My hope was that just like Luke was able to coax Anakin to re-emerge from the depths of Vader, I could get Jason to come back to the geek side. It was a great plan in theory, but in practice I was too scared to do any coaxing. So instead I followed him around, scared absolutely shitless about what would happen if Mom and Dad knew I was—gulp—smoking cigarettes.

There were two places on Feldman Road where we easily spent most of our days and nights: the Blocks and the Well Field. The Blocks were just that, three large cement blocks on the side of the road, blocking automobile access to a dirt road that led to nowhere in particular. The Blocks were in plain sight and we'd sit there, sweating it out at midday with cigarettes in hand, talking about absolutely nothing.

The Well Field was home to a large tree that we'd sit in or under, doing exactly what we did at the Blocks, except that we were set back in a cornfield and not sitting mere feet from the road. I always preferred the Well Field because of the guaranteed concealment it offered, especially after one terrifying incident at the Blocks.

On one particularly swampy Saturday afternoon Jason, Greg, and I sat drilling through a pack of butts at the Blocks as a pair of cyclists came riding toward us. Cyclists, with their aerodynamic spandex getups, were easy targets for discrimination, especially to thirteen- and fourteen-year-olds whose knee-jerk insults included sophisticated taunts like "fag" and "homo." So we stood there, leaning on concrete, sucking tar and smoke and stink into our young, pink lungs as these cyclists came ripping down the road. Greg—the tough son of a bitch he was—puffed out his chest and yelled down to them.

"Spandex warriors suck dick!"

We all laughed. Then they got close enough to see clearly and my worst fear came racing my way at a steady clip in all of his spandex-clad glory. My father was a cyclist. As were his friends. They cycled a lot. So much so that there was a good chance that if it were a Saturday or Sunday afternoon in Rowley, the weather was appropriate, and you saw some cyclists, you were probably looking at my dad and his friends. I flicked my butt into the dirt, stomped on it, and began to reflect on a life that was probably about to end before its time. Jason and Greg caught on a second after I did and tucked their cigarettes behind their backs.

"Hey, Tone," Dad said as he sped by.

"Hi, pal," his friend John echoed as he followed close behind.

The three of us swallowed big, hard cartoon gulps and waved like idiots. Speaking for myself, I can attest to very nearly shitting my pants. Then we hopped on our bikes and went directly to the Well Field. We did not pass Go and we did not collect a new pack of stolen smokes.

I had narrowly dodged a certain death, a fact that should have sent me screaming home, never to set foot down Jason's street again, but it didn't. I continued to let myself stumble deeper into a hole of poor judgment and adolescent angst, hating every minute of it.

Nearly getting caught smoking by my old man clearly wasn't enough to teach me a lesson. I was still spending every day with Jason and the gang. Most nights too.

"I think they're asleep now," Jason whispered as he eyed the ceiling under his parents' bedroom. "Be quiet. We're going out."

As we crossed his lawn and headed toward the street, we heard a window open above us. We froze, then turned slowly to face what I was sure was his mom or dad.

"Where the hell are you going?" It was Jason's older sister.

"Out. Got any bruins?" Bruins were the code word we used for cigarettes when grownups were around. His sister tossed a near-empty pack of Basics down from her window.

"You owe me!" she demanded.

"Shut up, and don't tell anyone you saw us."

A couple of houses down, the guys—Jeff, Greg, and a bunch of others—were standing around the side of the road, lighting up and waiting for us.

"Okay," one of the older, unknown kids declared, "let's get to it!"

Of all of our late-night time-killers, the most popular was whipping rocks or chunks of broken pavement at streetlights. Typically by the third or fourth shot one of us would take out the bulb, sending shattered glass and our victory cheers to meet each other somewhere in between the street lamp and the road. That night, despite my old, ironic nickname, I pitched a dead-eye shot and busted a light on the first try.

"Holy fuck!" Jeff said, cigarette hanging off his bottom lip to maximize his look of shock. "Pacitti fuckin' nailed it!"

"I guess I've been practicing."

"Practicing, my ass," said Greg, too big a douchebag to even give me the one shed of credit I was ever due. "Homo hit a lucky shot. Big fucking deal."

By the time we reached Jeff's house, we'd all grown tired of breaking stuff—all except for Greg, who needed to smash something juicier. Jeff lived across from a garage and a big empty lot that housed dump trucks and plows and a few other random cars, all of which were fenced off by chain-link topped with barbed wire. Being scrawny and thirteen, Greg got on his belly and managed to worm his way under the fence.

"Hey, where you going, man?" I asked. No one else had noticed that he was crawling under the fence.

"Shut the fuck up and watch!"

"No, really man, what are you going to do?"

"What else have we been doing all night?" He was on the other side of the fence now and was picking up a decent-sized rock off the ground. "Now stop being a such a fag and let me know if you see any cars coming."

I watched as he ran across the parking lot. It was around midnight, so odds were that he was safe from being spotted by any casual motorists. Like a white-trash ninja he climbed silently up onto the car hood and hoisted his rock up over his head. He sent it smashing down through the car's windshield, making a sound that was too loud for his own good or anybody else's. That got everyone's attention, and by everyone, I mean the rest of the guys, and the neighbors who were probably wondering what the noise and sudden lack of street illumination were all about.

"Dude, what the fuck?" someone yelled, starting a chain reaction of pissed-off responses.

"Greg, you homo!"

"Fuck this. I'm going to bed!"

We all scattered like the cockroaches we were, assuming that the sooner we made like the little cherubs we weren't and pretended to be asleep the sooner all would be forgotten.

Within a week the cops were in my driveway asking about the incident.

"Sir, where were you last Thursday evening?" the officer asked. To his credit he didn't seem like he was trying to make a thirteen-year-old shit his pants. Rather, it was just an unfortunate side effect of his being a cop and my being guilty.

"I, uh, Jason's? I was at my friend's house. Jason's house."

He asked me to confirm Jason's address, then added, "Are you aware that a car windshield was smashed that night at 10 Feldman Road?"

"Yessir." When I revealed that I knew what this was about, out of the corner of my eye I saw my father tense up. His body language suggested he would only wait until the officer was out of earshot before he ended me, and not a second longer.

"Can you confirm who did this?"

"N-no sir, I can't. All I saw was a shadow, you know, like in a movie where you can't see the person, but you can see a shadow? I didn't know any of the other kids there. Only Jason."

He seemed to buy it, which was surprising considering how poorly I had sold it. Mom and Dad had the truth out of me within ten minutes of the officer leaving our house.

"Do you know how that feels?" Mom asked. "A police officer coming to my front door asking for you!"

"What the hell were you doing there?" Dad growled through gritted fangs. "What the hell's the matter with you?"

I broke down. The truth and the tears tied neck and neck as they gushed from my face.

"We were just walking up the street, hanging out and minding our own business," I sobbed, "when suddenly Greg just randomly decided to smash a windshield!" Okay, so maybe the truth wasn't coming out 100 percent. I may have been destined for deep shit that day, but I wasn't about to dig myself any deeper by confessing to our streetlight-killing spree.

"What were you doing out so late?" Mom asked, almost begging.

"Yeah, what the fuck were you doing out that time of night?!"

"I don't know."

"You don't know."

"You don't know?!"

"I'm sorry."

Dad continued to glare at me, his eyes all fire and brimstone. He was seething. I imagine this is what he would have looked like if he knew I was smoking that day he rode by me. Thankfully he was not currently wearing neon spandex. Mom had her hand over her mouth, the gears chugging away in her head as she mulled over what her son had done.

"I can't believe you lied to a police officer."

"I know."

"Oh, I know you know." She paused, her internal jury reaching a verdict. "You're grounded. No TV, no video games, no phone. Three weeks. And I don't want you leaving the neighborhood."

I accepted the punishment and looked quickly at my father, seeing in that instant the savage bloodbath that was playing beyond his eyes. Projected on the big screen of the old man's bile-churning brain was a slide show of me being drawn and quartered. Shot before a firing squad. Strapped to railroad tracks while he twirled a Snidley Whiplash moustache. I would have welcomed any one of those punishments at that moment. Anything would have been better than the misery I was enduring under the rabid stares of four angry parental eyeballs.

They finally got up to leave my room. Before Mom closed the door, she turned to me one last time to deal the killing blow.

"We're very, very disappointed in you."

I knew that. She knew I knew that. She just said it because she wanted to rub my nose in it. If my mom were a *Mortal Kombat* character, the words "I'm disappointed in you" would be her Fatality and the sound of them uttered would cause your heart to explode in your chest, spraying blood and bone and self-loathing across the game screen.

I was never able to figure out how the cops got my name, but at the time I assumed Jason or his folks had given it to them. It broke my heart a bit thinking that was the case. I hadn't covered Greg's ass for his sake; I'd done it for Jason's. No one ever spoke about the interrogations we'd all gotten beyond asking simply who was questioned. I think it was because the rest of the guys didn't care.

"Fuckin' pigs," they said, and then went back to trying to black each other out with choke holds.

The week and a half of punishment—Mom let me out early on the grounds of good behavior—gave me time to move on from the horror of my first run-in with Johnny Law, but I was still quite shaken up by the whole thing. Maybe the guys were too. But they didn't strike me as the types to give much of a shit about what the police thought, then or ever. All of them except Jason, who I hoped was just as shaken up by it all as I was. But he didn't really seem to be bothered either by the situation or by being defined by the company he kept.

Who was I to talk? I was by no stretch of the imagination a pothead, then or ever, but at the time I wove their freak flag kinda-sorta proudly. And while I may not have bought into it, other people bought that I bought into it. One classmate actually called me a week after eighth grade got out and asked me if I could sell him a dime bag. Even better—or worse, depending on how you look at it—was the time that Queef asked me to roll him a joint using dried-up maple leaves and notebook paper.

"You hang out with all those potheads," he said as he handed me the materials for what was easily one of the lamest things I've ever made. I rolled, and he toked. Passing the maple leaf joint over to me, he stated proudly: "Dude, I'm totally getting something off this!"

"Bullshit, man, they're leaves. You don't 'get something' off of leaves."

"Come on, Nolan, I'm seriously getting a buzz here! Take a fucking hit, man!"

After a brutal stare-down, which I lost to the superior firepower of Queef's goofball grin, I caved. I smoked a maple leaf spliff rolled with CVS brand notebook paper. How could I have played such an instrumental role in something so profoundly stupid and not partake? The whole incident stands out as the lowest point in my accomplished career as a fake stoner.

But while I faked my way to a bad reputation, Jason was firmly cementing himself as one of junior high's official reefer delegates, complete with a big marijuana-leaf patch sewn on to the back of his hat. I don't know who he thought he was fooling. Certainly not my mom, who years after the fact made a comment about it. I believe her exact words were, "I don't know who he thought he was fooling. Certainly not me!"

By the beginning of eighth grade, Jason had an electric guitar and was playing Pink Floyd tunes like any good fourteen-year-old with a guitar and a taste for weed. He wanted to start a band. He'd play lead and Greg would be on drums. All they needed was a bass player.

"Hey, Tone, you should get a bass, man," Jason suggested one morning in homeroom. Jumping at a chance to keep up with Jason for as long as I could, I asked my parents for a bass guitar for Christmas. It was a black-on-black Fender Squire bass, and even though I'd had no interest whatsoever in playing bass before Jason told me to get one, I fell in love with it. Music theory would always dance outside my grasp, so I never learned to play it well, but I learned to play music I liked competently enough. Between Queef's own bass experience and weekly lessons from a local guitar Jedi I became somewhat mediocre at playing Metallica, Rage Against the Machine, and Floyd tunes. I also managed to develop enough of an ear to figure out how to hack my way through some simple, exceedingly lame original compositions.

Our band, Big Jay and the MVs—where, no joke, the MV stood for Moist Vaginas—never really happened. We got together to play once, maybe twice, in Greg's garage.

"So, what should we play?" Jason asked.

"I can play 'Money' by Floyd. I know half of 'Hotel California,' and I can play most of *The Black Album* and Rage's self-titled," I said as I tuned my bass incorrectly.

"I can keep a beat, so play whatever the fuck you want. I'll play it," Greg bragged.

We dicked around on our instruments for a bit and learned that Greg couldn't actually keep a beat and that Jason and I didn't know any of the same songs from the mutual albums we could "play most of." Eventually we got bored, smoked half a pack of cigarettes, and wound up back at Jason's house in front of the PlayStation. Greg and Jason may have even been high the whole time, but I wouldn't have been able to tell. Rarely was pot ever smoked in my presence, though it was always there in spirit. By that point I had still only smoked pot once, and I had never gotten high. I didn't even know what high felt like. It was lucky for my reputation that the kids I hung out with picked up my slack.

On April 20—4/20, the stoner equivalent of St. Patrick's Day—Jason skipped school to get baked out of his melon. The rest of us showed up for class, only to have the bubble of safety at school popped by the news that two guys in Colorado had gone off the deep end and shot up their high school. Word spread quickly about what had happened at Columbine, and by the end of the day the mood in my school's hallways shifted noticeably. Columbine became an ominous shadow that hung over school, and none of us really knew what to do with ourselves. Things were funeral-quiet for the rest of the day. Our world had suddenly become so much more dangerous, despite the distance between Massachusetts and Colorado. It was emotionally close, aesthetically close. The hallways of Columbine High were Triton's hallways. The Columbine shooters, with their trench coats and musical tastes, were just like kids we all knew. No fingers were pointed, none that I knew of, at least, but I can only imagine that some of my classmates started suspecting that others might actually snap. The line between fact and fiction seemed blurred. It was a scary time to be a kid.

We mourned together, feeling the evil presence that had forced its way into our collective hearts and minds. For me, school was a scary place to begin with, a place where you were judged in a glance and were torn apart with words. But not bullets. Suddenly junior high's caste system no longer mattered. There were bigger things out there than name-calling and being the weirdo.

That next day Jason didn't quite know what the hushed doom and gloom was about.

"Jeez, what'd I miss?"

"Didn't you hear?" I asked him.

"About what?"

"About the shooting? The high school in Colorado?"

The only thing he had watched on TV the day before was *Teletubbies*, through smoky, bloodshot eyes.

"Shit," he said. My brief summary of the shooting had killed whatever was left of his 4/20 buzz. I realized at that moment that of all the things to pretend to be, I had chosen to pretend to be a fourteen-year-old burnout, and I couldn't do it anymore. The days of me and Jason seemed like they were about to be cashed.

CHAPTER 11

JAR JAR BINKS AND HIS AMAZING HYPE MACHINE!

EIGHTH GRADE WAS WINDING TO a close. After sticking it out with the stoners and the dirtbags in hopes of retaining what precious little was left of the friendship Jason and I once had, I was more than ready for the year to be over. As a reward for my emotional suffering, eighth grade would end with the release of *Star Wars: Episode I—The Phantom Menace.*

For the life of me I can't remember which movie I saw it with, but when I first gazed upon the trailer for *The Phantom Menace*, I shat a brick. The happiest brick, in fact, that I had ever shat to date. Seeing the originals, my favorite movies ever, on the big screen had been nearly enough for me to say, "Okay, kill me now. Nothing in life will ever get any better than this." But a new Star Wars, one to call my own, like kids had had twenty years earlier? If it hadn't been for the promise of two more to follow, I'd have strapped on my Nikes and drunk that Kool-Aid so damn fast that the rest of the geek cult would've gotten wise to the scam and bailed in a glorious, Star Wars–fueled mass suicide. Goodbye, cruel world, and hello, Hale-Bopp. Next stop: Tatooine!

On my wall was a picture cut out of *Cinescape*—a sci-fi magazine Mom and Dad had given me a subscription to for several Christmases in a row—of Liam Neeson's Qui-Gon Jinn clashing sabers with the demonic-looking Darth Maul. This picture was attached to a countdown sheet I had made and pinned up, crossing off each day that passed from May 1 to May 19. If there was an article about Star Wars, I read it. If there was something on TV about the new movie, I watched it. This was the moment my whole life had been leading up to. This was the day that my dad had hinted at so many years back. Anakin Skywalker was about to become an actual person and not just an abstract, mythical presence. Jedi would be everywhere. These were the good old days, unfolding before our very eyes instead of in our imaginations.

In the trailers I saw glimpses of things and places I had already come to know from the holy texts of the Expanded Universe. The congested, bustling city planet of Coruscant was just as I had envisioned it when reading Zahn's *Heir to the Empire*. Darth Maul's dual-bladed lightsaber harkened back to Exar Kun, legendary Sith Lord and corruptor of Kyp Durron in the Jedi Academy trilogy. The prospect of a young Obi-Wan living up to his title of General in the Clone Wars was nothing to shake a stick at; nor was seeing the Force wunderkind Anakin Skywalker doing the heroic things that made his fall to the dark side so tragic. I was beyond hungry for this movie. I lusted for it. If the movie had been a woman, I'd have had a restraining order slapped on me for following her around, peeking in her bedroom window at night, and rubbing off in the bushes.

The night before *Phantom Menace* opened, I read the *Boston Globe*'s review, expecting the page to be gushing with the kind of words appropriate to what was surely going to be the greatest movie of all time.

"Amazing!"

"Spectacular!"

"An orgasm for the eyes!"

"The best Star Wars yet!"

"Cream-your-jeans sci-fi excitement!"

Instead the *Globe* gave it two and a half stars.

Surely they must have changed the ranking system so that now the best you could get was two and a half stars. I checked carefully, and it was not the case. The rating system was still based on four stars, so clearly it was a misprint. Yeah. Misprint. Had to be.

Film reviewer Jay Carr suggested that the movie just barely cut it. That while it was all sorts of awesome to look at, there was nothing intelligent happening to complement the visuals. It was, he said, basically a two-hour commercial. The movie critic whose opinion I valued so much when it came to learning about every new movie I never actually got to see was telling me that after twenty-two years in the oven, the new Star Wars movie the last thing I had expected to find: a turkey.

Screw that guy! What does he know? I tossed the newspaper down, disgusted that some hoity-toity film snob would dare look down his nose at my beloved Star Wars. *George Lucas couldn't possibly drop the ball as much as Carr had suggested. No way. Just wait until a legion of true believers saw the movie,* I thought, *and then he'll be eating the words he so carelessly committed to print.*

The spring air—normally smelling of new grass and blooming flowers and full of the sounds of birds—was alive with the collective excitement of a nation. The energy buzzed like lightsabers. It was so palpable you could grab a fistful of it, hold it, chew it, and scrub those hard-to-reach places with it. The Force became real on that day in mid-May. It surrounded us kids, penetrated us, and bound us all together.

The mounting anticipation for *The Phantom Menace* was a welcome reprieve from worrying about my friendship with Jason. For the first time in months, we finally had something to actually talk about. The fears I kept to myself about how the two of us were losing touch had been silenced during the couple of weeks leading up to opening day. A part of me feared that things probably wouldn't ever be the same between Jason and me, but for the sake of savoring the moment, that part of me kept to itself and let us enjoy something we had been waiting the span of our entire friendship for.

"I can't believe this is happening," I confessed.

"Been a long time coming," Jason said as he sketched an American flag with pot leaves for stars in his notebook.

"What do you think, man? Is it going to live up?"

"Dude, it's fucking Star Wars. What's to doubt?"

At the end of the school day, David, Jason, and I had a free period in the library, and *Episode I* was all we could talk about.

"It's going to be great," David declared matter-of-factly.

"Oh yeah? That's not what the *Globe* said."

"Screw the *Globe*. I read the novelization last week. I'm confident enough in it to know that it'll be great."

Some of us were lucky enough to have snagged tickets in advance. All we had to do now was wait impatiently for that goddamned 2:13 school bell to ring. Others weren't so lucky, and they shook like junkies hoping that a dealer would show up in time to supply their fix. We all shuffled around like zombies, speculating about what was going to be the coolest part of the movie.

"Dude, did you see that guy with the double-bladed lightsaber?"

"What about those space chariots?"

"For the love of God, when will the bell ring?!"

The only eye contact I made that afternoon was with the clock's face while I watched the last fifty-five-minute period shrink away, one deafening second at a time. When at long last the bell fired off like a starting gun, my classmates and I raced to our buses. At home, Mom was waiting to take me and a carload of friends down to the Liberty Tree Mall's brand-new, top-of-the-line, stadium-seating-and-everything movie theater. The place was packed wall-to-wall. Everywhere I looked I saw them: Han Solos, Obi-Wans, nonspecific Jedi Knights, stormtroopers, Vaders, Boba Fetts. You name them; there they were, smiling like jack-o'-lanterns. You could tell they were grinning through their thick plastic helmets, because their elevated cheeks made their Imperial-issued headgear sit a bit funny on their heads. Inside the theater was total pandemonium. It was like the scene in *Gremlins* when the monsters were packed into a movie house, raising hell during *Snow White and the Seven Dwarfs*.

As the lights dimmed and the advertisements for local car dealers and dentists faded from the screen, the audience broke into a deafening roar. Whistles and screams peppered the sound of a wave of applause crashing against the rocks of a two-decade wait. Popcorn and M&M's rained down from all sides. The jubilation in that room in the moments leading up to the start of the movie reached a level I've never experienced before or since that day. All signs indicated that I was in the middle of what could modestly have been called the greatest day of my life.

After a few moments the cheers faded . . . and nothing happened. There was a hiss and a crackle and a voice came out over the intercom. "Uh, sorry for the holdup, but if you don't mind, could you please shut off your lightsabers? Especially you guys in the back row. It's gonna interfere with the projection. Thank you."

The crowd exploded again with laughter as we looked around to see the dozens of red, green, and blue plastic lightsabers that had been waved proudly overhead for the last fifteen minutes. They were quickly shut off and tucked into the Jedi robes that so many moms had made so many Halloweens ago. The lights went dark and the previews rolled. We chomped at our fingernails while we waited for that familiar drumroll to introduce us to the first new Star Wars movie in many of our lifetimes.

The theater went from quiet enough to hear a pin drop on Endor to exploding as loudly as the Death Star when the titles whizzed by. Even the cheers I'd heard at the re-releases paled in comparison. I sat grinning, my eyes welling with tears, as a text scroll of new, unfamiliar words crawled up the screen. Over the next two hours, I was bombarded by new faces, new voices, new sights, and new sounds. It was like a first trip to New York City—it's a brand-new experience, but it feels familiar because you've grown up with every street, alleyway, and skyscraper shown on the big screen. This was Star Wars, there was no doubt about it, but now we were seeing parts of it we hadn't been shown before. Some parts were good, like the podrace, Qui-Gon Jinn, Darth Maul, and a Galactic Republic not yet fractured by Sith tyranny. But then there was Jar Jar Binks and midi-chlorians.

Jar Jar was goofy, a trait that doesn't fit that well into a Star Wars movie. He was a bastardized cocktail mixed up in the Mos Eisly Cantina, with equal parts of DNA taken from Roger Rabbit, a Caribbean clown, and a salamander. Dick and fart jokes followed him wherever he went. Even at age fourteen, when a fart would send me to the floor holding my gut and laughing like a moron, these gags felt wildly inappropriate. And Jar Jar's voice, sweet merciful crap, his voice! Chewbacca grunted, growled, and roared his way through three movies, and Artoo spoke in chirps and beeps, but no one had a hard time understanding either of them. Their words—whatever language they were spoken in—were completely contextual, usually given in clear response to Han or directly translated by Threepio. Jar Jar was overtly cartoonish and too over the top for something as serious as this particular space odyssey.

The midi-chlorians—a plot twist that offered a scientific explanation for the existence of the Force—would manage to overshadow even Jar Jar's presence. Star Wars is magical, just like the Force. And saying that a Jedi didn't actually get his power from the mystical energy that forged the galaxy but rather from a bunch of microbes took that magic away. It was like learning that your parents were really Santa Claus, or worse yet, proving or disproving the existence of God. Proof goes against the point of faith. The Force didn't need a scientific rationalization, just faith, and explaining that away with science sort of spit in the eye of Luke's struggles to become a Jedi in the original trilogy. Suddenly I got the feeling that he didn't have to believe in himself or overcome all of that adversity; he just had to read an instruction manual It snapped me out of the moment and derailed my attention on the movie when even Jar Jar hadn't been able to shake me loose of the stranglehold the film had on my undivided attention.

Even with Jar Jar and the magic-stealing blood bugs, I still loved the movie. Loved it with a capital L-U-V. Qui-Gon was a badass, the outsider Jedi Knight willing to defy the likes of Yoda and Samuel L. Jackson to bring in the most powerful being he had ever come across: Anakin Skywalker. Ewan McGregor, cast wonderfully as a young Obi-Wan Kenobi, had all the charm and energy that Alec Guinness had breathed into the character's older iteration.

The podrace was hands down one of the coolest thing I'd seen on the big screen outside the original movies. It was *Ben-Hur* meets the speeder-bike chase in *Jedi*. Watching Anakin in action was proof positive that he was Luke's father. No one else could handle one of those machines as skillfully as a Skywalker. The crashes, the sabotage, the whole damn thing just dripped with that Star Wars feeling, trumped only by the beyond-epic duel at the end between Darth Maul, Qui-Gon, and Obi-Wan. These were Jedi like we'd only read about them in Expanded Universe comics and novels. They were the samurai of the stars.

The scene was pushed into the realm of supercool by the music. That booming and ominous choir tapped into everyone in the audience and struck the same emotional chords that the theme song and "The Imperial March" had. I shot up when

Qui-Gon got impaled by Maul—absolutely beside myself at the thought of losing him so soon after the new trilogy started—and had to restrain my excitement when Obi-Wan, fighting to keep his anger in check after the loss of his master, dealt that mortal blow to Maul, severing him in two.

As the credits started to roll, I sat back, a big, satisfied smile on my face, and thought, *You did it, George. I don't care what that dillweed Globe critic said; man, you hit it out of the park.*

After the movie we headed to the food court to eat our weight in fast food. Jason, David, and I gushed through mouths full of French fries about the amazing feast our eyes had just taken in.

"Holy crap," Jason said, his language cleaned up on account of my mom's presence. "How cool was that podrace?"

"I'm just going to say it," I added. "This ranks as my third favorite in the series. *Jedi* just got bumped."

Let's be honest here: for me, at fourteen, to rank any of the Star Wars movies was just an excuse to further break down my all-time favorite thing ever. All the movies existed on their own plane, a cinematic Elysium unto themselves. Our expectations had been met with flying colors. Star Wars was back, and nothing could change that now, not with two more movies coming our way. But despite David's prescreening enthusiasm, he was not impressed.

"I don't know," he said, his face projecting the obvious disappointment he may have been trying to conceal for the rest of our sakes. "It was just . . . some parts were really stupid. Like Jar Jar? Come on, man!"

"Well," my Mom chimed in, enlightening us with some criticism from before any of us were born, "people felt the same way about Yoda when *The Empire Strikes Back* came out."

Like the mob of harrumphing fanboys we were, Jason and I backed her up, but David wasn't sold.

"Well, okay, Yoda then. He's supposed to be like 900 years old. If this was thirty years before the other movies, how come he looks so much younger? Thirty years shouldn't make much of a difference. Plus, he sounded like Grover! And Obi-Wan said that Yoda had taught him. Why's Qui-Gon his master all of a sudden?"

That one hurt. All that Yoda stuff was true. I tried to argue that maybe, as the head of the Jedi order, it could be assumed that that's what Obi-Wan had meant.

"Besides," I added, confident that I had the case-winning defense at my disposal, the kind of line that bad TV courtroom dramas build up to, "Obi-Wan also told Luke that Vader killed his father, then argued that from a different point of view he was telling the truth."

David furrowed his brow, groaned, and kept his comments to himself for the rest of the day. Ten years later he prided himself on being the first one to call it like it was: *Phantom Menace* was kind of a turd. I was just too hung up on what it was in the most basic, superficial sense—a new Star Wars to call my own—to see that.

I didn't see *Episode I* again until about a year later. The Star Wars hype had faded, and the shuffling of light and dark side decks had stopped once and for all. With the book of junior high finished, I began a new chapter of life. Despite the deep-seated, unconditional love I had for Luke, Han, and Chewbacca, I had to take a step back and sort of turn away from their galaxy.

Once high school began, Jason became too busy with guitars and weed to do much else, so we spoke almost exclusively in the one class we had together. *Episode I*, in some strange twist of fate, didn't bring with it the new era of Star Wars fandom that I had expected, at least not at my school. Instead it seemed to mark the end of my more innocent youth—and the end of my friendship with Jason. Welcome to freshman year.

CHAPTER 12

BETWEEN HEARTBREAK AND *EPISODE II* THERE IS AWKWARD TEENAGE ROMANCE

DURING THE FIRST WEEK OF the year my bass guitar led me to a classmate named Johnny and to a new group of friends who had what he called a band. Johnny was something of a Renaissance man at our school. He existed in every strata of high-school society, always had a seat at every single lunch table. He was a musician, an artist, a superstar athlete who played a sport each season. He was a clown and a scholar and the darling of just about every faculty member in the school, and not a single kid resented him for it. As the creative driving force for this band, Johnny took it upon himself to introduce me to the group.

"Don't you want to, I don't know, hear me play first? Like an audition?"

"No no no," he insisted. "I've heard you play bass for Big Jay and the MVs." *How the hell did he hear about that?* "As long as it won't be interfering with your commitments there, we'd love for you to play bass for the Missing Children."

I explained that due to unspoken creative differences, Big Jay and the MVs had disbanded and no reunion tours were in sight. Just like the MVs, this new band didn't actually exist, at least not as a band so much as a clique. Of the eight or so of us—yes, eight people and not even a single mediocre bass player—Johnny and I were the only ones who knew how to hold our guitars the right way, and playing them was another thing entirely. They were a group of kids who were more interested in teen angst and melodrama than space operas, and since they worshipped things and people like Korn, the Crow, and Tim Burton movies (which they only worshipped in a superficial sense and not out of any appreciation for the films' cinematic merits), my heroes from a galaxy far, far away became objects of my own private fascination.

On a Friday night early in the school year, Johnny invited me over "to jam" and meet the rest of the gang/band. I was the first to show up, so Johnny and I listened to the new Rage Against the Machine album and goofed off on our guitars while we waited for everyone else to get there.

"They made us wait three years and the best they can come up with is a track called 'Mic Check'?" Johnny balked as he read the liner notes for Rage's *The Battle of Los Angeles*. As the metal funk and Zack's oppressed howling cranked out of the speakers, the doorbell rang and Johnny ran to get it. Stevo vaulted through the door, tackling Johnny like Hobbes tackles Calvin.

"Tony, this is our leader-slasher-singer, Stevo. Stevo, this is Tony, our new bass player."

"Sweet! We need a bass player, dude. Do you like Korn?"

"Uh...."

"Bizkit?"

"No thanks, I ate before I came over."

"Godsmack?"

"Oh! Have we been talking about music this whole time?"

Within the hour the rest of the gang showed up, and our jam session quickly devolved from Johnny and me playing what few songs we each knew separately to bombing at trying to play something together. It wasn't long before I was trying to undo Stevo's attempt to drop tune my bass while I watched my fellow bandmates have a half-assed mosh pit in Johnny's parents' basement. It was kind of awkward, but not nearly as awkward as when someone wrapped Stevo and his girlfriend, Karen, in a string of Christmas tree lights and we all watched them make out during an excruciatingly long cut from Rob Zombie's *Hellbilly Deluxe* album. These kids were weird. But I was weird too. Plus, Stevo seemed to like me, and he called the shots.

Stevo was a scrawny little spaz whom I had known from our eighth-grade math class, though at that point he still held a special place in my heart as that guy who called my house looking to buy weed from me. He was always decked out in huge, baggy black pants adorned with long, menacing wallet chains, and that night was no different. He had a different Korn shirt for every day of the week, accessorized with his studded wristbands and collars, and he was at least four other types of academically recognized "in your face." A poster child for Hot Topic—home to every miserable teenager's overpriced, angst-ridden apparel needs—he announced his approach with the clinging and clanging of his accessories before you ever saw him coming. His outlook on everyone else around him was just as black as his wardrobe, and despite preaching that we should all be comfortable with who we were, he was extremely narrow-minded about anyone who wasn't one of us.

"Look at those fucking jocks," he'd sneer on days before a football game, in between doing his best Jonathan Davis impression and making out with his identically dressed girl-friend. "Bunch of fucking dumb sheep."

"You know Johnny's on the team, right?" I'd point out as the only other semi-functional musician in our band accepted a plate of brownies from a cheerleader.

"Johnny doesn't count, man, he likes the Pumpkins." It was during those couple of years with Stevo and the Missing Children—the name of our fake band—that I settled into my very angry, post–*Phantom Menace* rut. I hated the world for not giving me a fair shake, but to be perfectly honest, I was surrounding myself with people who didn't seem to want their fair shake. We hated you for no other reason than our assumption that you didn't think outside the box. We were "artistic" and "different" and didn't like Top 40 radio. (Stevo turned a blind eye to Korn's frequent appearances on MTV's *Total Request Live* countdowns and the top of *Billboard* charts.) We were everything we claimed to hate, and we didn't even know it.

Behind my anger was fear. I was scared to show the world around me who I really was, afraid of rejection. Fear had most certainly led me to a dark place, despite all the warnings that a very wise old Muppet had been giving me for years. Yoda was still there for me, but I was no longer listening.

We did nothing to make ourselves stand out other than dress funny, and I couldn't even do that right. In one ill-fated effort to be more goth, I bought what I believed were a pair of black jeans to show the world just how miserable I was.

"Dude, I thought you said you got black jeans?" Stevo asked during a break from making out with Karen in the hallway.

"I did, man. I'm wearing them right—aw, fuck!"

"Yeah, man, dark blue isn't black. Try not to be such a poseur, huh."

Between my not-gloomy-enough wardrobe and a soft spot for Everclear, something no goth would ever admit to, I knew that goth living wasn't going to be for me. So I let them keep the label goth and settled for the more universal Reject as my own professional title. Honestly I never really had my heart in it. Stylewise, I was only ever a casual metal kid who dabbled in the realms of punk and skater, all of which was built on an uneasy foundation of geek chic.

Despite their store-bought doom-and-gloom appearances, my new friends were extremely excited to have me join their gothy little mob, and I was happy they would have me.

"Tony!" Stevo would proclaim every morning when we met up in the hallway. "Mother fuckin' Tony-Wan Kenobi!" Stevo and his mutants were a means to finally settle into some sort of clique.

David and I still hung out, but we would soon start to drift, and my new choice in friends served as a catalyst for that. They were wrapped up in self-loathing, self-made drama, and how little the world thought of them, stuff that I could commiserate with, but not everyone could.

"You can tell me honestly: look me in the eye and say that these kids don't take themselves a bit too seriously?" David asked. "That hanging out with them isn't like a living soap opera?"

"Dude, Stevo and Karen are going through some pretty serious shit right now," I argued in defense of my new friend.

"He cheated on her with their best friend, but it totally wasn't his fault; it was hers!"

"Karen's?"

"No, the other chick. The whole thing's fucked!"

"How is this not proving what I just said to you?"

I was so into the idea of having a group of friends that I couldn't admit that David had a point. If I burst the bubble on this clan, how could I be sure I could find another one to accept me for what I was or was trying to be?

David never really gave a shit, at least not as far as I could ever tell, about what other people thought of him. He was proud to the point of being stubborn, and his extreme pride clashed with people just as much as our forcing the idea that we were fuckups. Once my new crowd became a more permanent fixture in my life, David and I started to part ways. By the time he decided he was transferring to a private high school, I felt I had to act as if I resented it. I knew I had caused a rift in our friendship, even if it was unintentional. As much as it hurt that he was going to leave, I didn't feel like I had a right to let him know.

When David told me he was leaving after our sophomore year to attend a private academy, all I could ask him was, "Why?"

"Because I don't feel challenged here," he told me. "Because I want to get into a really good college and I want to be able to show that I have what it takes." It was the only genuine excuse I ever heard personally for going to private school. Most kids I knew who went did so because it was like buying a name brand. It was Pepsi, not the supermarket's generic, 85-cans-for-three-dollars-brand cola.

"Well, good luck, I guess." That was the closest I came to apologizing for putting our friendship on the back burner.

As time passed after *Episode I* was released, I found myself teetering more and more on the fence about it, especially because of David's outspoken disapproval of its subpar return to the galaxy. Rewatching the old ones only made me question *Phantom*'s merit even more. Though I still defended it for the most part, I was no longer so sure of its ranking as my third-favorite Star Wars movie. It wasn't long until it came out on VHS, and after seeing it a second time, I came to a verdict: I didn't really like *The Phantom Menace.*

I was at a crossroads with both Star Wars and life. Old friends were fading away and my movies were changing radically before my eyes. I was becoming bitter, allowing an internal darkness to take hold of me. I felt betrayed for the first time by Star Wars, the one thing I had never imagined capable of betrayal.

To get over this first case of heartbreak I turned to the opposite sex. After all, a woman might break your heart, but at least she might love you back. Until high school, girls had frightened me, and an utter lack of faith in myself had kept me from even thinking about attempting to ask a girl out. I had several crushes throughout junior high and the beginning of my freshman year, but outside my circle of friends, my experience talking to chicks was laughable. I'd have had better luck discussing *The Phantom Menace* with Alec Guinness's ghost through a Ouija board than trying to make small talk with an actual live female.

Within our little group there were four girls. One was Stevo's girlfriend, Karen. Two of the other girls fell into the just-friends category. So that left Liz. She had the unique ability to never keep her opinion to herself. She was headstrong to the point of being stubborn, a trait that, at first, didn't clash with my juvenile sense of humor and soft-spoken wit so much as it complemented it. As Liz and I spent more time hanging out together in our group of friends, we started to develop a strange rapport: I'd make a joke, she'd shoot it down, and I'd shrug off her comments with an ever-sarcastic smirk. It didn't hurt that I thought she was all kinds of cute—long brown hair, green eyes, and an impressive cup size (at fifteen, that last part holds more weight in developing a crush than it ought to). All of the inhibitions that had had their stronghold over me seemed to vanish completely, at least when Liz was around.

One weekend we all sat in Liz's basement huddled around a small stereo listening to Korn CDs and a tape I had recorded of myself playing Metallica tunes on my bass. Though everyone was very encouraging of the one member of the band who knew how to—sort of—play his ax of choice, Liz was particularly impressed.

"Is that really you playing?" she asked.

I watched her reaction while my clumsy rendition of "Call of Ktulu" filled the air. It sounded like a bass guitar experiencing a series of puberty-induced vocal cracks.

"Yeah, that's me. I played it and recorded it myself."

"Wow."

"Yeah, but you know it's a Metallica song. I didn't write it. But on the other side of the tape are some tunes I wrote."

"Awesome. I can't wait to hear them."

That day I joked with her, teased her, and pushed every button I didn't know existed, and she just volleyed it all right back at me. We had become the only two people of any importance. Picking up on our less-than-subtle banter, one of the other girls wrote, "Liz likes Tony" on a blackboard that was set up in the corner of the basement.

"No I don't," Liz whined, her smile giving away what her blush couldn't hide. Then she looked at me and shyly added, "Really, I don't."

That's when it dawned on me that yes, what we had just spent the last few hours doing was flirting. I don't know where I learned how to do it, but I wasn't about to argue. Since I had never tried my hand at winning over a girl before, the interactions I had with Liz left me feeling drunk for the rest of the weekend. The more I thought about it, the more I realized that I kind of liked her and would like to ask her out. I confessed this to Stevo, but the whole thing was terrifying. To ask a girl out required a certain kind of stuff that I didn't think I had, despite what was obvious to everyone else in that basement: she totally liked me back.

Walking out of English class a couple of days later I heard the unmistakable sound of clanging wallet chains as Stevo came running full speed down the hallway. As I turned to greet him, he grabbed me by the shirt and slammed me into a locker.

"Dude!" He screamed it in my face, his lips curled back into a big Jack Skellington grin, his eyes bugging out of his head. "Remember how you told me the other day that you liked Liz?!"

I panicked.

"Fuck, you didn't tell her—"

"She likes you too! She told me!" He let go and sprinted toward the cafeteria shrieking, going out of his way to be as flamboyant and different as he could, like always. I just stood there, knees clickety-clacking, ready to barf all over the place.

Sitting at our usual table in the cafeteria—back in the corner, away from all the jocks—I sat putting all the pieces together, weighing my options and devising a killer battle plan to sweep her off her feet. With a deep breath I made my move.

"Hey," I said casually, "Karen, can I talk to you a sec?"

Karen moved down to the far end of our table with me, as far away from Liz as I could get.

"What's up?" she asked, her silly grin revealing that she knew exactly what was up.

"Look, I want to ask Liz out, but I'm probably going to puke all over her if I do. So . . . you know . . . can you ask her for me?"

Karen's silly grin morphed into one of pity. She smiled because she had to. Her forced smile masked what she had to have been thinking: that I was a dweeb who, if I kept this up, would die alone.

"Sure. Yeah, of course I'll ask her out for you," she said. Admiral Ackbar would have been ashamed.

While the girls whispered, blushed, and giggled, I sat at the end of the table wondering why I ever thought Liz would like me in the first place. What did I have to offer her? I was a thoroughly paranoid, fairly pasty string bean with a bad haircut that my parents still picked out for me. My sense of humor leaned toward jokes involving genitals, assholes, and all the things that came out of them. I wanted Star Wars to be real life. I had never kissed a girl, and even if I had I probably would have been bad at it. I had no discernable skills unless you considered self-loathing a talent, in which case I'd be captain of the school's varsity self-loathing team. And what if I ever came face-to-face with a situation where it called for me to defend the honor of my beloved? A pre-confidence George McFly could have made me his bitch. And Liz told Stevo that she liked me? Clearly the poor girl had become confused somewhere along the line.

After a sequence of worst-case scenarios raced through my head—the tamest of which involved Liz, decked out in a Thuggee headdress, ripping my beating heart out of my chest, setting it on fire, and burning the school down with it—Karen came back over to my end of the table.

"She said yes," she told me, her smile only slightly less patronizing.

"Oh."

"It's so great, isn't it? You guys are so cute!"

Karen went back to sit next to Stevo, who had a large portion of his lunch chewed up in his mouth and was ready to feed his girlfriend like an incestuous mother bird. As I tried really, really hard not to pull a Stan Marsh and projectile-vomit across the table, Liz got up and sat next to me.

"Hi," she said with a shy, rosy-cheeked smile.

"H-hey," I looked at her quickly and smiled back, then looked back down at the lunch I hadn't started yet. I picked up my bologna sandwich, ripped it in half and offered it as a first gift to my first girlfriend.

"You want half a sandwich?"

Just like that we were suddenly in a serious, totally committed relationship. By checking the box next to "yes," she became my girlfriend and I was her boyfriend. It was that simple. That's how love was handled when I was fifteen. You ask a friend to ask a girl out for you, she says yes, and you awkwardly hug each other goodbye at the end of the day while all of your friends watch you like you're a couple of snuggling zoo chimps. *Awww, they think they're people!*

Liz and I began to date, though I'm not sure that dating is quite the right word for it. We didn't go on any dates during that first year and change, at least not on our own power. Spending any time together was dependant entirely on whether or not my parents could drive me to her house on weekends or pick me up after taking the school bus home with her. I was constantly reminded of my dependent state.

"Did you drive yourself to her house, pick her up, and take her someplace?" Dad asked one night at dinner after I had referred to one of my days with Liz as a date.

"No, you dropped me off at the movies and she met us there."

"Then it wasn't a date."

As far as teenage romances go, ours was a series of a few awkward firsts that were all overthought on my part. I had no faith in myself, but I was 100 percent sure that Liz was going to be my wife some day. I was madly in love for no other reason than that she was my first girlfriend and that's how I was supposed to feel.

Everything I did with Liz was part of an equation that had to be executed precisely for fear that the whole thing would fall apart. I've since learned that a romance has to be allowed to grow naturally. At the time I ran everything through a rigorous gauntlet of half-baked pseudo-science and what TV had told me was "romantic." I planned, weeks ahead of time, when I was going to kiss her for the first time and when I was going to tell her I loved her. Both came nearly a month after we started dating, which shows just how big a wussbag I was.

Despite all my airtight love algorithms, I somehow thought our first kiss should deserve the ever-romantic setting of a busy school hallway after last period. Even worse was that, I wasn't even planning on kissing her on the mouth for the first go-round, but something in me, something that probably wanted to kick my own ass, made me do it at the very last possible second.

"I'll call you tonight," I told her, "after dinner, okay?"

"Yeah, but don't wait too long. If *Buffy*'s on, I won't answer."

"Yeah, okay." And then I went in for the kill.

It was quick, a peck at most. Certainly no tongue. I probably had nasty, cracked lips and Cheetos crumbs on my face, and as usual, the whole gang was standing around and watching. That's what we did. We watched each other make out.

Through the tiny crack I allowed one of my eyes to open I nervously watched Liz's face for some sort of reaction. All I saw was a blushed, red blur before she threw her arms around my neck and I buried my face in her shoulder.

"That was nice," she whispered.

"I think I love you," I confessed. She pulled back from me, her face alight with the giddy luminosity of a fifteen-year-old supernova.

"I love you too!"

You'd think the knowledge that a girl loved me would be enough for me to sack up and be a man about things. Instead I found myself, to steal an excerpt from the review for Spinal Tap's 1974 album *Intravenous de Milo*, "treading water in a sea of retarded sexuality." It took me five months to work up the nerve to put my tongue in her mouth, a moment punctuated with all the class and romance you'd expect to find in front of a high school while a bunch of audio-video geeks, junior varsity wrestlers, and perpetual detention-hall residents waited for the late bus.

After our lips parted I was coated in a flop sweat. *Did I put my tongue in too far? Did I move it around enough? Did she taste my lunch? Had any little food bits left caked between my teeth gone bad since lunchtime?*

"Did you like that?" I asked. I was constantly looking for feedback. I should have printed out an evaluation form for every first move I made. Under the comments section she could have written, "Tony is surprisingly adequate a kisser for someone who has up until this point only used his tongue to make fart sounds and lick nine-volt batteries. I do stress adequate, but once he overcomes his own lack of confidence and allows himself to just experience 'the moment,' I'm sure he will upgrade to quasi-proficient. C/C+."

My issue was that I was caught between the howling, banshee masses that were my raging man-child hormones and any sense of propriety about "how a gentleman acts" that my parents had tried to instill in me.

"A gentleman doesn't do anything to make a lady feel uncomfortable or taken advantage of," I'd hear my mother tell me as my hand fumbled with Liz's bra.

"Do you want your dick to look like a cucumber and fall off? I don't want grandkids yet! Wear a condom!" my father bluntly instructed across the chasm of memory, as I never once made it anywhere close to needing to use a condom.

A gentleman also doesn't keep a secret briefcase full of porno mags in a secret fort in the woods that was built solely for housing it, but I did. I was no gentleman. Deep in my core there was an animal lust clawing to get out, but like a Jedi I was able to keep my dark desires in check.

At their worst, these feelings never amounted to anything more than trips to second base and the never flattering, mutually embarrassing dry hump. But between my bumbling attempts at physical intimacy were a series of sweet, if not entirely naive, first-love moments. An old journal I kept is riddled with proclamations of undying love and my pining for my distant—she lived two towns and fifteen minutes away—lover. But pining for what? I never say, but when we talked on the phone, we generally just listened to each other breath. I can't think of a single conversation we ever had. But at a time when it seemed no one else gave a shit about us, we had each other. At a time when I was angriest with the world, when I would hear Metallica's "Until It Sleeps" on the radio and break into tears and tell my mother that I felt like James and Lars had written that song just for me, I had someone who told me that she loved me every day. For the time being, it was enough to make me feel like I could take on the whole Empire myself.

CHAPTER 13

(W)RITE OF PASSAGE

BY THE BEGINNING OF OUR junior year, Stevo and Karen finally ended a yearlong will they/won't they saga of trashy teen TV proportions and broke up for good. With the group's self-appointed co-captains walking away from one another, our gloomy fellowship fell apart. Liz and I stayed together, but we were on and off of speaking terms with different members of the group at different times. It didn't change how we felt about each other, but no longer feeling like I was tied down to Stevo's silly, fifteen-year-old outsider's ethos started to open some doors for me. I was starting to make friends with people I normally wouldn't have spoken to. It was through one of these new friendships that I got the ball rolling that would finally knock me out of my shell.

Every year during the week leading up to Thanksgiving, my high school held Spirit Week, which consisted of a series of goofy events and contests to determine which class loved our high school the most. At the end of the week, all of the competitions were tallied up and capped off with each class putting on a skit. I had started to get a very small reputation as the kid who wanted to be a writer. Based on this rumor, a class officer named Lindsey approached me with a strange proposition.

"So we're going to start homecoming stuff soon, and I was wondering, you know, if you were interested, if you'd maybe write our skit this year?"

Such a thing would have never, under any circumstances, have crossed my mind. I was scared shitless about sharing my writing with friends and family, never mind the in-crowd and their faculty supervisor.

"Do *they* know you're asking me to do this?" I asked, assuming that if I agreed and she told them I was in, the bottom would completely fall out and leave me feeling all sorts of bad for myself.

"It's cool. I told them you're very funny—and they seemed to buy it." She was obviously joking, but I took her words at face value and assumed she had to lie about my credentials. I was still flattered, and I felt that if I didn't say yes, I'd be as lame as I assumed everyone thought. Plus, my sudden ego told me I could do it better than it had been done in the past.

The skits I had seen my first two years of high school were pretty much the same kind of lame. They contained a bunch of paint-by-numbers pop-culture references, elbow-nudging jokes aimed at the faculty, and the occasional bad musical number. I wanted to do something different, something that people had never seen before. I also knew that I had a certain responsibility. As an outsider, not in the broad-stroke sense that Stevo and our miserable goth gang had considered ourselves, but as someone who functioned outside the social circles that tended to run these events, I was a new voice on the homecoming stage. I had a chance not only to represent, but also to finally entertain, a sizable chunk of the student body that historically loathed these kinds of things.

I knew I couldn't make it a niche thing. I had to please everyone, to pull a Luke Skywalker by coming out of nowhere and blowing up the metaphorical Death Star.

My skit centered on a guy who wanted to be a cheerleader. The only problem was that nobody liked him. He was made fun of and picked on when all he wanted to do was be a part of the big Thanksgiving game. After he was left behind on game day, he met a homeless man who had tried to be our high school's first male cheerleader a decade before. When he had failed, it had left his life in ruin, but my hero wasn't about to let history repeat itself. Despite adversity, he pushed on and helped win the big game.

It was a tale of understanding and acceptance. As Lindsey read my dialogue out loud to the assembled group of students and faculty advisors after school, nausea and his old pal paranoia decided to pay my gut a visit. Suddenly I was nine again, being asked to share my work with the class. The class officers, advisors, and other kids involved genuinely seemed to like what they were hearing, but I still wanted to kick down the door and run out of the room screaming.

"Tony, this is great," Lindsey said after she finished reading. Her opinion was backed by several smiling, nodding heads.

The class officers, advisors, and other kids involved really seemed to like it, a reaction that left me more than a little shocked.

"I agree. This is really a very amusing skit," echoed our class advisor. His voice was a deep monotone that never, under any circumstances, revealed any sort of genuine interest or excitement. In what I like to think was a conscious move on his part, he chose his words very carefully so that they too hid any shred of interest in what he was talking about.

"I'm sure that your fellow classmates will be just as entertained by this as we all have been today," deadpanned our supposedly entertained advisor. Roles and production assignments were doled out and for all intents and purposes we were beginning to bring my skit to life.

The feeling of accomplishment and belonging was intoxicating. It had come from the unlikeliest of sources, people whom I had blindly assumed had no interest in a geek like me, people whom I had written off as a bunch of those John Hughes-ian "cool kids."

Something I created had been accepted. I started to feel like I might know who I was and what I wanted to be. And sometimes when things are going smoothly for the underdog, controversy strikes.

After about a month of prep work, a gay kid from the senior class got wind of our cross-dressing hero—I'd thought it would be funnier if my protagonist wore a girl's cheerleading uniform—and called foul on us.

He walked up to me in the hallway on Halloween, dressed as a trashy drag queen. "I heard about the skit you wrote," he told me, his hands planted firmly on his hips as he shot me the stink eye from behind layers of slutty-looking makeup.

"What about it?" It was hard not to stare at the tissues stuffed lumpily into his tube top.

"I think it's horrible. As a homosexual I find it deeply, deeply offensive."

"Yeah, but my character's not gay. It's not a gay joke at all."

"You're wrong. You're wrong, and it's homophobic and it's mean."

I would have socked him if I didn't think it would have looked like I was hitting a girl, and I was certainly brought up better than to hit a woman, regardless of any amount of stubble that may be showing from under her rouge.

"I think you missed the point, man. It's supposed to be a thing about understanding and everybody accepting ..." I became frustrated, not so much by his complaint but by how he was voicing it. "Look, is there another gay person I can talk to about this?"

"You're not doing this skit," he yelled, jabbing a rather well-manicured finger into my chest, adding, "I will see to that, even if it's the last thing I do!" He stormed off on a pair of high heels that he was surprisingly adept at maneuvering in.

His complaint reached the top brass, and by the end of the day, the assistant principal had called me into her office to discuss what was quickly becoming a bit of a situation. She claimed she had asked several faculty members to read over my skit and their reviews were less than flattering.

"They said that they found every word to be offensive and appalling," she informed me, "and I tend to agree with them." My fingers tightened around the arm of my chair.

"What I think we have here," she continued, "is a case of a person—you—who has been picked on by others throughout his life and is trying to seek revenge via what is supposed to be a fun event. Not only do I think that this is not the proper forum for such a thing, but I think that you may want to consider seeking some kind of counseling."

Luckily Lindsey was there to jump in and argue rationally on my behalf when I was too worked up to speak. The fact that this woman had swept in and pulled the plug on something I had worked so hard on was one thing. But to suggest I was trying to use homecoming as a vehicle for my own personal revenge—and on top of that suggest that I needed to see a shrink—pushed me right over the edge. My inner Wookiee wanted to pull her arms out of their sockets and beat her to within inches of a fair compromise with them. But the vice principal's mind was made up, and she couldn't be swayed. Any work we had done over the last month was for nothing, and homecoming was coming up fast.

"Fuck it!" I told Lindsey as we made our way to the parking lot. "I'm out."

"You can't do that," Lindsey pleaded.

The way I saw it was this: the kinds of people the vice principal told me I was attacking not only liked what I had come up with but were actively involved in its performance. I wasn't about to waste any more of my time with it if all I was going to be met with were labyrinths of red tape and wild accusations about my emotional stability.

"You can't just quit."

"Yes, I can."

There was a pause.

"Then quit. Quit and they win."

I wrote this off as a lame line, something you'd be more likely to find in a televised after-school special than in a real-life after-school discussion. But the more I thought about it, the more I knew she was right. When I got home that afternoon I left my homework in the car and got right to work on a new skit. After about five hours I sat back, looking at a pile of scribbled pages, and called Brian.

Brian and I had met on the afternoon that *Episode I* was released by way of mutual geeking out in the library. Though that was our introduction, our friendship wouldn't begin until a heated argument the next year over whether a fighting game—*Soul Calibur* for the Sega Dreamcast—could ever be good enough to merit winning the Game of the Year award. Before long we went from talking smack about video games in study hall to spending most weekends skateboarding, wading through stacks of comics, and watching *Rocko's Modern Life* bootlegs in fifteen-hour chunks. We became a tag team; he was the more reckless though goodhearted Artoo to my uptight, paranoid, and less fabulous-looking Threepio. To warp an old turn of phrase, we were two droids in an escape pod. "Dude, listen to this and let me know what you think," I told him after explaining the mounting controversy.

I read him my new script, which was a parody of late-night talk shows, complete with a band, guests, and a Letterman-esque top-ten countdown. The first "guest" was the school's head of disciplinary action, a guy whom everyone thought looked like Superman, a gold mine for easy laughs. The following guest would be our principal, Jason's uncle, whom I portrayed as a laid-back dude who cared less about school policy then he did about getting his garage band off the ground.

"So," I asked after Brian and I had talked out some details, "you want to be the host?"

"Dude, if this is gonna stick it to that chick who complained about your first skit then I'm there."

"It was a guy, actually. He was just dressed as a chick."

"Same thing!"

The next day I pitched the idea to the skit actors. It received unanimous approval, and we started casting and rehearsing immediately. A class officer was cast as our Superman-looking faculty member, and Mackie and a couple of our musically inclined acquaintances made up the band. Since Jason's uncle was a character in the skit, I decided it was given that Jason would be asked to play him. He and I had gone through the better part of our freshman and sophomore years saying next to nothing to each other outside of school, but at some point in the beginning of junior year, we started to talk again. There were no sappy "I missed you, man" exchange or talks about lost time; it just happened as naturally as our friendship had begun when we were in the second grade.

"I hear they're making a new Turtles movie," Jason said.

"Yeah, I heard that. Have you seen the *Attack of the Clones* trailer yet?"

"Only eighteen times!"

And just like that, we were the same goofy kids we had been back in elementary school. Having Jason in the skit was like having a much-needed straight-block fall into place in my cluttered game of *Tetris*. When it fell, the mounting stacks of regret and having nothing to say to one another disappeared, opening the game screen for all sorts of new possibilities.

The production was polished and ready to impress the heck out of the school. The big day came and I was nervous as hell, but things went off without a hitch. Every joke landed its punch, everyone nailed their lines, and Brian and Jason stole the show. It absolutely killed. The crowd—my teachers, my peers, my friends—was laughing at words that I had put down on paper.

After the skit the assistant principal approached me. I was braced for the worst.

"That was very funny," she said, her gag reflex very noticeable as she forced out a compliment.

"Thank you."

"Yes. . . ." She paused to allow the tension to build. "It was much more appropriate than that first thing you wrote."

She extended her hand and brought her backhanded congratulations to a close. As we both walked away, I couldn't help but wonder what had happened to that poor woman to make her so impenetrable to anything remotely fun or pleasant. Had she witnessed every dog she ever owned get mowed down by trains and bread trucks? Maybe she was a robot.

Regardless of any traumatized-by-gratuitous-puppy-death robots who may have stood in my way, the skit began a new era for me. I wasn't Joe Cool by a long shot, but I had cemented myself as a person and a voice that mattered, and I did it on my own terms, even if I faced a bit of creative persecution along the way. If anything, it made the skit's success that much sweeter. I proved to the people who opposed me that not only could I play ball, but I could play it better than any of them—or even I—had ever imagined. I felt like a somebody for all the reasons someone should feel like a somebody. I had earned it.

I was getting there. I was finally starting to feel like the person I wanted to be. I was this close to being as content as a guy like me could be in high school, but as far as I'd come at that point toward being happy with my life, there was still one accomplishment I had yet to achieve—I had not sat down to watch a Star Wars movie with my girlfriend.

Liz had never seen any of the Star Wars movies and had written them off as too lame to bother with, a claim that made no sense coming from a girl who was a rabid geek for *Buffy the Vampire Slayer*. Also to her detriment was the fact that she cited Nerf Herder as her favorite band but didn't even get that their name was a Star Wars reference. This was unforgivable. Aside from their sick band name, there's no reason to claim Nerf Herder as your favorite band (though in the interest of giving credit where it's due, "Van Halen" was a pretty good tune).

For two long, agonizing years I begged and pleaded and bartered and bent over backwards to get her to watch a Star Wars movie. Finally, one afternoon during the spring of our junior year, I got Liz to sit down and watch *Empire* with me. The day was eerily similar to the first time I watched *Empire* myself; Mom was even ironing in the same spot.

"Well," I nervously asked as the closing credits started to roll, "what did you think?"

"Yeah," she said. "It was good. I liked it."

I was shocked. I was afraid I had built up Star Wars to the point where she wouldn't be able to enjoy it for what it was, never mind for what it meant to me. But it worked. She actually liked *The Empire Strikes Back*. At the end of the movie, Liz could barely contain her laughter, she was so overcome with joy. At least I thought it was joy. What else would it be? I had just introduced her to the greatest movie of all time. I started to wonder at her mirth, and just to be safe, I asked her why she was giggling. She looked at me through teasing eyes and spilled the beans.

"I've seen it before," she confessed with the greasy smirk of a trickster devil-goddess strung across her lips. "I just liked watching the way you'd squirm when I said I hadn't."

In my head a record player scratched to a halt. Liz, my own girlfriend, led the Imperial assault against what had over the years become my own personal Echo Base. I dumped that bitch within a week.

Actually, there needs to be some clarification. I didn't dump her because of Star Wars; I dumped her because of a cup of iced coffee a couple of days later, but the Star Wars thing definitely lit this particular powder keg's rapidly shortening fuse.

I stopped at Dunkin's to pick up a coffee every morning before school, and one morning the caffeine went right to my head. I was in a good mood, bouncing off the walls and just loving life. I bounced my way into school and saw Liz.

"Hello, my dear! How are you on this most wonderful morning?" I asked, thinking that a girl would be psyched to see her boyfriend in such a good mood.

"What's wrong with you? You're acting kind of stupid," she responded with all the excitement you'd expect to find in the voice of someone who was annoyed on an intrinsic, cultural level.

It was in those words, "You're acting kind of stupid," that certain feelings I had been having lately started to come into focus. A part of me was beginning to think that there was more out there. I'd think this when I lay in Liz's room reading comics because she'd fallen asleep immediately after we got home from school. It was starting to dawn on me that Liz and I had little in common. That she had become the boring sun that my disinterested planet revolved around out of habit. She was whiny and narrow-minded and stubborn and controlling, and above all else, she was holding me back. I had finally started to open up, to be myself and to make new friends, but being with her made me second-guess everything I did. I censored myself before I said anything in her presence, always afraid of the repercussions. I Couldn't say "fuck" when Liz was around. Couldn't make an off-color joke or threaten to hang my ass out of a window and take a shit on the hood of a buddy's car when Liz was around. Couldn't fart. No long, one-sided discussions about Star Wars or comics or video games. Nothing.

I was at a point in my life where I was making friends as opposed to just finding people to commiserate with. Friends who laughed at my jokes, enjoyed my company, and liked what I liked. Dare I say I was kind of, sort of, maybe somewhat a little bit cool, and all I had done differently was start acting like myself. Or as Liz had put it, start acting kind of stupid. Bullshit! She was acting kind of stupid!

She was the one part of my life that didn't feel right anymore. For two years we had stuck it out. We were each other's best friend through a lot of that hard, figuring-out-who-you-were stuff that a lot of people had to go through alone in high school. However, what it all boiled down to was that we weren't meant to be with each other, despite what a less-confident me had once believed. We were going through the motions, and I was finally confident enough to realize that I didn't have to settle for that anymore. She was *Episode I* all over again. I couldn't live in denial about *The Phantom Menace*, and I couldn't live in denial about her. I had filed my VHS copy of *Episode I* away and never looked back, and now it was time for me to dump her.

The rest of the day played out like a stereo system with the business end of its speakers pressed firmly into a mattress. Everything was murky, dull, and muffled. My teeth ground down to the gums as I stalked from class to class, trying to contain the urge to scream. Anger was the first step to the dark side. I didn't want that. I was on the brink of liberating myself, of finally breaking through that last flimsy wall of reservation and self-doubt, and I wasn't about to reinforce it with a public temper tantrum.

At the end of the school day, Liz and I walked miserably to my car, a '95 Jeep Cherokee named Dolores. Dolores, whom I had named after Bob Hoskins girlfriend from *Who Framed Roger Rabbit*, was a beautiful shade of R2-D2 blue. I always felt like Han Solo driving that thing. Weaving through traffic I'd hear the asteroid chase music in my head. I loved that car, and all the accidents and problems I had with it only secured its spot in my heart as my very own *Millennium Falcon*.

I took Liz to my house to break up with her, which was not the cleverest move. We should have gone to her house so I could have done it straight up and left. Instead I took her fifteen minutes out of the way of a more-convenient, less-awkward post-breakup ride without my soon-to-be-ex-girlfriend in the passenger seat.

Just as our relationship had been riddled with that sappy, "I wuv you more" stuff, our breakup was full of the same kinds of played-out clichés.

"No, I still love you, but just not that way. I love you like a . . . a really good friend. Or a sister," I said. All lies. "Of course I still want to be your friend." No I didn't.

"I'll always be there for you." Blue ribbon winner for 2002's Meanest Thing I Could Have Said Ever award.

As she sat there crying, telling me how awful a human being I was, I couldn't help but cry a bit myself. It was the first time I had ever caused someone that sort of pain.

"What am I supposed to do now?" she begged. "I love you!"

All I could think to say was "I don't know what you're going to do now. But I don't love you like I thought I did, and I can't be your boyfriend anymore."

I had never really understood the harm my words could do to someone's feelings. I wasn't ready to be so upset myself about our breakup, and at the time I would rather have stabbed her in the head than have to be the one to tell her one more time that I really didn't love her anymore. Maybe I should have asked Karen to dump her for me.

After all the crying was over, after I was told how terrible I was to do such a thing, there was an eerie calm. Liz wiped her eyes and took a deep breath, and I waited for the sounds of bulging muscles and snapping bones that would preface a rancor exploding out of her skin, ready to rip me to shreds like so many of Jabba's doomed, dancing slave girls. Instead she exhaled calmly and looked at the PlayStation 2 I'd bought the week before.

"Why don't you show me this *Grand Theft Auto* game you've been talking about."

Tens of digital miles, several million dollars in property damage, and twelve dead virtual ladies of ill repute later, I drove her home, speeding the whole way there. I just had to get her out of my car. The whole "let's play video games" thing after I had supposedly torn her heart out was driving me nuts. We had absolutely nothing to say to one another on the ride home.

When I got to her house we looked at each other, said our goodbyes, and gave each other one last, big hug. I smiled, she smiled back, and I pulled out of the driveway nice and slow until I saw that she was inside with the door closed behind her. Then I put it to the floor and bombed over to my friend Dan's.

"Hey buddy!" he said, surprised by my unexpected, frantic knocking on his front door.

"Dude, I just broke up with Liz. Wanna hang out?"

If I was the go-to Star Wars guy, then Dan was the go-to comic book guy. I had just become interested in comics, and Dan became my Obi-Wan. He was also the go-to guy for lady troubles, because Dan's life was a revolving door of girls, relationship foul-ups, and uneasy reconciliations. It was Dan who discovered that if you throw Kermit the Frog's "Rainbow Connection" on a mix tape for a girl, then she's "guaranteed to make out with you." His advice on coping with a breakup was just as prophetic.

"Man, when you break up with a girl, there's only two things you can do—LEGOs," raising a second finger, he continued, "and comic books."

We sat in his room and talked out the highlights of my first breakup. While I tried to maintain an air of civility about the whole thing—I didn't once use the term *dump* because it implied it all came from a mean place—Dan was appropriately uncivil about it.

"It had to happen, man," he said as he clicked blocks together into an intergalactic battle-tank. "We all saw it coming. We were just waiting for you to get the hint."

"But it just felt so shitty to have to do that to—wait a minute, what do you mean you 'all saw it coming'?"

"Tony. We didn't like Liz. At all. Fuck, half the time we were afraid to call you just because we figured she'd be with you."

I was shocked. After letting it all soak in for a minute, the first honest thing I'd said all day roared out from behind a curtain of self-imposed faux tact.

"Well why the hell didn't you say so before, man? I could have gotten this shit out of the way sooner!"

"You had to figure it out on your own," Dan mused. "No one can tell you to dump your girlfriend—yes I said 'dump'—unless she's like, I don't know, smacking you around or something."

I stewed over what Dan was saying and hated the fact that he was right. Had my friends all told me what they were waiting for me to find out, that I was trapped and needed to break myself free of a suffocating situation, then I would have hated them. Knowing how stubborn I am, I might have even not broken up with her out of spite. It's one thing to hear that your best friends hate your girlfriend after you've dumped her. It's another when you've told yourself that she is your sole reason for waking up and dragging yourself to homeroom.

"Come on," Dan said. "Let's go for a ride."

A quick ten-minute drive up the road and over the New Hampshire border was our mecca, Chris's Comics. It sat on the end of a small shopping strip that included a fireworks store, a smoke shop, a pawn shop, and an adult bookstore called Leather and Lace that featured twenty-four-hour live peepshows. It was one-stop shopping at its finest. Liz had always hated when I'd stop by the comic book store after school before going to her house. I mentioned that, and Dan let out a long, irritated sigh.

"Man, if she couldn't keep her mouth shut for a quick stop on Wednesdays for new comics, then, I guess dumping her was just for the best."

Inside the store I took in a deep, healthy breath of newsprint and ink and basked in my surroundings. Chris's Comics has that smell of musty old paper, like an attic or a basement full of dusty old toys you had long forgotten about. Even if I don't leave with anything, I love just being in a comic book store, surrounded by the pulp heroes and the villains, the superpowered soap operas, and all the overpriced merchandise. In that shop I was at peace for the first time that day. *Everything will be fine,* I told myself. *Now you can move on and try to become who you really are. Plus you won't have to babysit an unappreciative girlfriend in a few weeks when* Episode II *comes out.*

CHAPTER 14

I, FANBOY

I WALKED INTO STUDY HALL one afternoon shortly before *Attack of the Clones* was released, whistling Monty Python's "Sit On My Face." The theater teacher, Mr. Quillinan, looked up from what he was reading and waited for me to notice that he was staring in my direction. Nervous, I looked around.

"What?"

Mr. Quillinan looked over his glasses and smiled.

"I know what you're whistling. Python's good stuff."

He hunched back over his notebook and stacks of folders, leaving me wondering whether I'd just been reprimanded for something. I cautiously watched him from behind my copy of *The Hitchhiker's Guide to the Galaxy* and was relieved when he leaned back, put his feet up on the desk, and pulled the newest issue of *Time* magazine out of one of his folders. Yoda was on the cover.

"Whoa! Can I read that when you're done?" I asked him.

"You're a fan, I take it?"

"Fan is a gross understatement."

Q, as we all called him, was just twenty-five at the time, and by all rights was a big, dumb kid like the rest of us. We'd chat through study hall and in between classes, breaking down the finer points of *Episode I*'s crap-factor and our hopes for *Episode II*.

"As long as there's less of that Jar Jar asshole, I'll be happy," Q pronounced as we walked to our respective next classes.

"Yeah, but even if he does show up, this Boba Fett precursor guy will make up for it."

Q pulled me aside from the shuffling masses of students and suddenly became very serious.

"Maybe you can shed some light on this. Why the hell does everyone like Boba Fett so much?"

"You're kidding, right?" Up until that day, no one had ever questioned Fett's obvious greatness. It was an opinion I assumed everyone subscribed to.

"Enlighten me. The guy stood around, did nothing, and then was killed by accident, all for the sake of a burp joke in *Jedi*. How is that remotely badass?"

"I'm guessing you don't buy the argument that he's the man who got Han Solo, do you?"

"Vader got Han Solo. Fifty bucks says that without the Empire at Fett's back, Han could've outsmarted him."

When we weren't arguing the virtues of the Star Wars secondary characters, we'd get into lengthy chats about filmmaker Kevin Smith—a more relatable hero than George Lucas, what with his whole fanboy-does-good persona—and soak our shirts with drool over Sam Raimi's soon-to-be-released Spider-Man movie. Q was the first adult aside from my parents who encouraged me to embrace my nerdy side.

The timing of our meeting was particularly fitting. Between *Episode II* and *Spider-Man*, May 2002 was a great time to be a nerd.

The end of my junior year, even beyond movies, was pretty monumental. Being single in the prime of my high-school years (even though I didn't really take any advantage of it) was liberating on a "We Just Blew Up the Death Star!" scale. For the first time in two years I was able to think all the thoughts I could ever want to think, and think them for no one other than myself.

My family was, as expected, sympathetic to and supportive of my breaking up with Liz.

"Your first break up isn't easy," my dad told me, "but you did what you needed to. You can't always worry about how the other person's going to take it."

Mom agreed but added that breakups, despite the implication in what Dad had said, don't ever get easy. Amanda, barely able to contain her excitement about the breakup, tossed her glee-shined two cents at me with a faux-mocking, "You could *probably* do better."

The last remnants of my goth gang from the first half of high school were now long gone, swept away like the remnants of the Old Republic. I didn't speak to any of them aside from Stevo, who was still stuck in his tunnel-vision ways. He had grown significantly and genuinely crazier than he had been when I first met him, thanks to his discovery of acid and the works of Hunter S. Thompson.

"Good God, man! How do they expect me to get all this algebra homework done with all of this bad craziness I'm subjecting myself to?" Stevo would bark during homeroom, high off his rocker and affecting all manner of Thompson-like body language.

"Couldn't tell you, Stevo," I said from behind an issue of *Batman*. "I'm knee-deep in bat country myself."

"Fucking swine!"

I certainly didn't talk to Liz anymore, despite any breakup promises that suggested I would do otherwise. The best thing to come out of that whole phase was a well-learned lesson in how not to get through life: depressed, with a soundtrack provided by Korn. Life was anything but depressing at that point. Damn it, life was good! I had friends I had a genuine connection with, not just friends I was trying to fit in with.

One Friday night a week or so after I had sprung myself from my dead-end high-school romance, the gang—Jason, Brian, Mackie, Dan, and me—kicked off this dawning of a new age right. We piled into the room above my parents' garage and assembled for a marathon session of *Quake III* on Dreamcast and *Time Splitters* on PlayStation 2. We played till our thumbs ached and our eyeballs nearly bled. We murdered the hell out of each other in gratuitous, oh-so-glorious displays of digital carnage, all while stuffing ourselves with junk food. We were seventeen and we sat on thrones crafted of comic books, guitar amps, and Nintendos.

With these friends I found the feeling of brotherhood and—gasp—even optimism that had long eluded me. There was no common ground with the stoners and the dirtbags, and all I had in common with the goth kids was a mutual sense of self-loathing. I had tried for so long to force bonds with forced friends that I almost missed it when it all came naturally. It was by abandoning my desperate search for camaraderie that I finally found it. That night was the beginning of our greatest days together. We were a bunch of geeks enjoying life's finer things: video games, comics, movies, and dick jokes. We hadn't a care in the world any more important than whether or not *Episode II* would live up to our hopes of being, at the very least, better than *Episode I.* If the previews were to be believed, that was going to be a sure thing.

The final days ticked by slowly. The bunch of us had all made our plans to see *Attack of the Clones* on opening day—as if there was really any other option—and since we weren't taking any chances, Jason and I had taken it upon ourselves to get everyone's tickets a week early. The woman at the ticket counter was easily 153 years old. Her hands shook violently when I handed her our money, and she seemed about as confused by the computer screen she was supposedly operating as you'd expect someone out of the mid-nineteenth century to be. By some miracle, she printed the tickets and handed them to me.

"Numbah nine on your left!" she croaked. Her voice properly reflected the ravaging effects of age, smoking, surviving the Great Depression, and the sadness of being the last living Civil War widow.

Jason looked nervously back and forth. "Is she talking to us?" Jason asked.

Slowly we backed away, not wanting to confuse her more than we already had by not following her instructions.

"Where are you going?" she demanded as we crept away. "I told you boys it was numbah nine on the left!"

Maybe she was just trying to be helpful by telling us where to go in a week when the movie opened. Or maybe she was dead and, only through some sick perversion of modern tech-nology and long-forgotten black magicks, was hooked up to the ticket computer, repeating in English the commands of zeroes and ones that it fed into what was left of her decayed brain. A zombie brought back from the grave so AMC The-aters could save a few bucks on labor costs. Once we were hidden within the veil of her cataract fog we made a run for the food court.

"So," Jason started as we sat down with our Quarter Pound-ers and McNuggets, "we've got a week left. Less. You still feel-ing good about this?"

For three years we'd all spent countless hours poring over every inane detail of *The Phantom Menace* and the special edi-tions in an attempt to figure out where something so right went so wrong. Choosing to show Anakin as a kid was frequently discussed, as was the film's boring economic policy–fueled con-flict. No one watched Star Wars for the heated senate hearings over sci-fi trade embargos.

"The way I figure it," I told Jason between big, greasy bites, "is that *Episode I* had all the ingredients, you know? But it's like someone read the recipe wrong. What we wanted was, like, a thick, hearty sci-fi chili, but instead we got, shit, I don't know. . . ."

"Raw haggis?"

"Exactly!"

Attack of the Clones, corny, drive-in creature-feature title aside, was looking like anything but a bunch of essential organs stuffed haphazardly into a sheep's stomach.

The trailers were ominous and mysterious, pointing only at big plot points and no specifics. Obi-Wan reported some-thing from an ocean planet about a clone army, and Palpa-tine ordered the formation of a Republic army. Yes! The first three films gave us a galaxy divided by civil war, and here it was again, not just some isolated skirmish like the one in the last movie. Obi-Wan and Anakin now seemed to have grown up to the point where we would see them as the heroes they were alluded to being in *A New Hope*, and certainly we would begin to see Anakin's flirtation with both the dark side and Padmé. All of this was suggesting a more grown-up, meatier Star Wars. Something to really sink our emotional and intellectual teeth into.

"Plus the new Boba Fett," Jason was sure to remind me. "Can't forget Boba fucking Fett, man." The idea of seeing a real Fett-versus-Jedi encounter—regardless of what Q might have thought—was enough to make even the most pessimistic of nerds drool all over their "It's a trap!" T-shirts.

Sitting through classes the day *Episode II* opened was like sitting through class in 1999 all over again, only this time with some strange new thing called self-esteem. Somehow I had managed to forget about all the mediocre things that had happened during *The Phantom Menace* that would make any sane person nervous about its sequel. That's because I wasn't a sane person. A person in love is anything but sane. To give yourself over to something so completely, to be willing to endure such mental anguish and to be so forgiving is the curse of a certified, love-struck loon. And brother, did I have a mean hard-on for Star Wars.

Yes sir, I had the itch again, that insatiable hunger for all things Lucas. History lessons and math formulas passed right through me like a proton torpedo through a thermal exhaust port's ray shield. My brain was on vacation, busy daydreaming of other planets and aliens and intergalactic war and mystical energies. There was no way outside of direct mention of Star Wars that I would give you the time of day. I whistled Yoda's theme through class, hummed the Cantina songs through lunch, and as I kicked open the bathroom door, I yelled, "Into the garbage chute, flyboy!" The day a new Star Wars movie premiered was like February 29, that beautiful, special day that only comes once every few years. Any fear that it wouldn't live up to my expectations was buried deep under a pile of embarrassing memories, anything I ever learned in Spanish class, and the acknowledgment that after dating a girl for two years, I was still a virgin.

Standing in line for our lukewarm lunch, the boys and I were noticeably antsy. We wanted to see that movie, damn it, not better our education. It didn't seem right that school would have the audacity to be open on the opening day of a new Star Wars flick. It was in this moment, when the levees of anticipation burst and our excitement flooded our conversation, that we all came to a painful realization.

"Why didn't we just cut school today?" Brian asked. "Seriously, what the fuck is wrong with us?"

"We're fucking geeks, dude," I told him. "There's probably some hidden programming in our brains that won't let us deprive ourselves of our quality public-school education."

"I don't know about you," Mackie chimed in, "but I don't think I've heard a teacher say a single thing all day."

"He's right," Jason added. "They all sound like Charlie Brown teachers. We're idiots. We should have seen this movie by now."

We were almost there. Just a couple more hours. We could make it. Two more classes, one quick car ride, and we'd be there.

When we pulled into the mall parking lot, we marveled at gaggles of fanboys dressed in their fanboy best.

"Whoa, sick Darth Maul," Mackie commented.

"Which one?" Brian asked.

As we made our way inside, Brian, Mackie, Jason, Dan, and I walked by at least four Darth Mauls, their costumes ranging from store-bought Halloween quality to super-authentic fanatical levels of detail. The legions of stormtroopers, Rebel pilots, and Jedi were back out in full force. The mall had once again been hijacked by fanboys and transformed into an impromptu Star Wars convention.

Inside the theater, ushers guided us up packed aisles with replica lightsabers the likes of which none of us had ever seen before. Extremely detailed hilts were topped with a column of super-bright LED lights that ignited in rapid sequence. When one lit up in the dark, you'd think an honest-to-goodness lightsaber had just been fired up. Seeing them made the thought of ever using one of those big, clunky lightsabers with the series of clear plastic cylinders that extend when you flick them seem beyond stupid.

"We need one of those," I said.

Jason corrected me. "No, we need, like, eight of those. Each."

The house lights faded, and I felt as if time had flashed back to three years before. All the thundering cheers happened in all the same spots, and when all was said and done we filed out to our cars just as smitten as we were before.

The bunch of us reconvened at Giovanni's, a sub shop down the street from the mall that had become our go-to eatery for post-movie consumption of the greatest sandwich known to man: a large roast beef sub with sauce and cheese.

None of us knew what the sauce was. We believed it to be some sort of barbecue sauce variation, but I'll be damned if anyone can find it outside the North Shore of Massachusetts. Later, while at college, I ordered a roast beef sub once—only once—and asked for it with sauce and cheese.

"What kind of sauce?"

What kind? There was an option? Giovanni's knew what kind of sauce I meant!

"Uh . . . barbecue?"

What I got was a sub roll packed with gray, inferior beef that had been slathered with some thick, brown muck. The kind of barbecue sauce they give you in little cups at McDonald's. It was gross. It was cold, and gooey, and gross. At Giovanni's the meat was warm, pink, and juicy. The sauce was a thin, red something or other that had just the right kick to it, and it all just melted in your mouth. It was the perfect complement to a most satisfying cinematic experience.

"Was it good for you?" *Episode II* seemed to be asking us as we stuffed our maws with submarine sandwiches.

"Baby, you know it!" we answered in so many words.

It was like a smooth, slow-burning cigarette after making sweet, sweet love to a beautiful woman. Or at least what TV and movies had told me to believe that a smooth, slow-burning cigarette after making sweet, sweet love to a beautiful woman might feel like.

We were all in agreement—*Clones* was better than *Episode I.*

"Like, by a landslide," Mackie stated.

There were a bunch of killer scenes, stuff like Anakin—who was finally old enough to mess an alien up, no questions asked—butchering that group of Sand People, women and children included, for killing his mother.

"There was just a ferocity to him," Mackie said. "So much hate. There's no doubt that that miserable son of a bitch is going to be the most feared man in the galaxy some day."

"Yeah, dude. Only Darth frigging Vader could be that brutal," Brian added.

"Yeah. Total badass. And fucking Jango Fett," Jason said. "Sam Jackson and Sam Jackson alone is cool enough to take him down, that's how cool he was. No better way to go out."

As the seething nerds we were, we all knew that Boba had a rocket pack, missile launcher, flame thrower, grappling hook, and who knows what else in that Swiss Army knife space suit of his. Seeing it all put to use in a throw-down with Obi-Wan Kenobi was pretty sweet if you asked us. No one did, but we told them anyway. And as for those seismic bombs Jango used when he was chasing Kenobi in the asteroid field—classic cool.

Yoda's lightsaber duel with Count Dooku was everything we'd hoped it would be. First the little guy proved that he lived up to his reputation by dominating with the Force. He caught and absorbed Dooku's dark side lightning.

"Caught it!" I yelled, slamming my hand down on the table. "Made it disappear in a little blip in the palm of his hand. It was like watching a girl tie a cherry stem into a knot with her tongue!"

When Yoda and Dooku cracked out their lightsabers I was wondering how things were going to go down, what with Yoda's being a whole three feet shorter than his adversary.

"Size," as the little guy once said, "matters not."

Jumping around like some Force-fueled chimp, Yoda made a lot of geeks' wet dreams come true that day, hacking and slashing at Dooku while he flipped and flopped through the air, bounding off walls and bringing his emerald green blade down with more power than any Jedi twice his size.

"I almost cried," Dan joked.

"Fuck you," I said. "I did cry!"

Episode II was so, so beautiful that first and second time I saw it, but as the weeks went on, the whole thing started to feel more like a one-night stand than true love.

There are certain things you look for in a girl and a movie, things that you know turn you on both physically and mentally, and I was realizing that just getting off wasn't going to cut it. I wanted this to be a Star Wars movie that, years down the road, I could still claim to love with all my heart. Instead I got a few cheap thrills the first couple of times we hooked up, but after that I didn't want to call *Attack of the Clones* back. Besides, she had such a stupid name—*Attack of the Clones*. The clones didn't attack; they came to the rescue. It was like calling back that hot, easy girl you had nothing in common with. You know she'll be all dolled up for a night on the town and you're almost guaranteed to get laid, but you know there is nothing going on behind those pretty blue eyes and that generous cup size—or in this case, crazy special effects and sweet-ass fight scenes.

Within a month it was obvious that "better than" wasn't good enough. "Better than" also got redefined, or at least its definition was precisely nailed down. "Better than" clearly meant very little of Jar Jar Binks. He had in fact been side-lined to two scenes, one minor and one major-ish. The bigger scene pinned him as the one guilty of nominating Palpatine for emergency power of the Senate, paving his way in the flesh and blood of the Jedi order to become the Emperor we all know and revile. Less Jar Jar wasn't enough, and the closer I looked, the more I found things that I didn't like.

The Phantom Menace, in what is probably a minority of an opinion, at least tried to stick to a vibe similar to the first three movies, even if ultimately it failed to recapture the magic. Instead of trying to fix what everyone hated about it, with *Clones* it felt like Lucas decided to overcompensate with shoehorned winks and nudges to the original trilogy and by showing off his seemingly bottomless bag of distracting special effects. For me that wasn't enough. I wanted to tell Lucas, "Don't try to win me over with some goofy space diner thinking I'll remember the Mos Eisley Cantina, or even more of a stretch, fondly recall *American Graffiti*. Don't have your villain look at Yoda and declare, 'It is obvious that this contest cannot be decided by our knowledge of the Force . . . but by our skills with a lightsaber.' You might as well have had Dooku look right at us, right through the screen, and say, 'Here it is, kids, the moment you've been waiting twenty years for! Hey Yoda, crack out that ol' laser sword, guy!'"

In the end it felt like it went nowhere. Cool scenes aside, nothing important enough happened. I felt like I had watched an entire movie consisting of nothing but background information. Weak sauce.

The final nail was driven into the coffin when I caught a commercial after the movie had been released showing clips of Yoda's lightsaber fight and declaring "Yoda Man!" (You know, like "You da man!"?) At least they didn't make Sam Jackson throw up a Black Power fist at the end of the Battle of Geonosis and yell, "Yo, right on, green dude! You a bad motherfucker!"

My views on the movie were dumped on anyone in earshot, though my parents seemed to have to endure the brunt of it. I made sure to give them plenty of warning before they got around to seeing it themselves.

"It's not that good," I warned them. "Guys, seriously, like, nothing happens. It just sort of shuffles around, people shoot at each other, then it turns into a gladiator movie. It's weak. Weak, I tell ya!"

"Oh, it can't be that bad," Mom tried to calm me. "You just expect too much."

"And with good reason!"

When they got back home from the theater I went on a rant, with my mom casually agreeing but still generally enjoying it. My father just shook his head and looked over his glasses at me.

"You're looking too much into this," he said, trying not to laugh at my being all red in the face and raving like a crazy man. "It's just a movie."

"This is not just a movie, Dad! This was the second blown shot of what was supposed to be a sure thing. If the Red Sox were up in the World Series three games to none, had a commanding lead by the top of the ninth in Game Four, then blew that game and the three that followed, would you really just sit there and take it while I said, 'It's just a game'?"

"First off, the Sox will never make it that far. Second, are you using sports talk? Do you even know what you just said?"

I ignored Dad's jab at my athletic illiteracy and stormed off, leaving him to laugh in his recliner. Some things are just guarantees, and this should have been one of them. *Episode II* should have been amazing. Just a movie? The old man was losing his grip!

A couple of deep breaths and a bit of time apart from *Attack of the Clones* and things were fine. I was in a good place. I had good friends, we were having good times, and high school was soon to be a rapidly fading spot in the rear view. My friends and I suddenly found ourselves in a world where the once-brutal hierarchy of high-school social life had all but disappeared. It was nothing at all like what *The Breakfast Club* and its strictly regimented high-school caste system had told me to expect. There was harmony, a balance to the Force that had always seemed like a pipe dream at best.

But for Jason and me, senior year and the summer that followed would be the last of our hurrahs despite the fact that neither of us left the state for college. We'd keep in touch throughout our freshman year, but after that we would talk less and less. When it happened, I couldn't take it personally the way I had before. Jason and I had drifted apart for the last time, each living the lives we had chosen for ourselves. Not knowing or expecting that things between us would fade away naturally was a blessing. Looking back, we couldn't have ended our own little saga on a better note. But at the time, the questionable endurance of our friendship was nowhere to be found on my mind. All I knew was that there were two more grand adventures coming at me hard and fast from the distance: college and *Episode III*. What college would bring was a mystery, but there was no way *Episode III* would be as bad as *Episode I* and *II*. Right? I mean, he saved all the good stuff for last, made it so he had to give us the goods.

Right?

EPISODE III

LOVE AND LIGHTSABERS

CHAPTER 15

ONE GIANT LEAP FOR FANKIND

AFTER HIGH SCHOOL, BRIAN AND I both attended the University of Massachusetts Dartmouth, the forgotten middle child of the UMass family. A typical discussion about college with a member of my extended family went as such:

Family Member: Oh, where do you go to school?

Me: UMass—

Family Member: (Excited gasp) Umass Amherst?! That's terrific! Great choice!

Me: Uh, no, actually, I go to UMass Dartmouth.

Family Member: Oh . . . well. Coulda shoulda, right?

My decision to go to the UMass that apparently no one liked was twofold. To start with, the film studies branch of their English department intrigued me. And upon taking a tour of the campus, Brian and I had come to the conclusion that with all of the stairs, rails, and sheer amounts of concrete,

UMass Dartmouth would have made a sick level in one of the *Tony Hawk's Pro Skater* video games.

During our sophomore year at UMass we took a trip up to New Hampshire for our first tattoos, an idea I had been pondering over for a year or so at that point. Most of the time I would kick the idea around with Brian, but sometimes I'd mention it casually when I was home for a weekend or talking to my parents on the phone. Mom and Dad's usual reaction was a moment of contemplative silence followed by knee-slapping laughter.

"You'll never do it," my old man taunted.

"You hate needles. You don't do well with pain. What do you think it's going to be like?" Mom threw in.

They laughed. They laughed it up good. Finally, after several dinners where I was apparently the funniest thing they'd heard in a while, my mom managed to ask me a serious question.

"So, what do you want to get?"

"A Star Wars tattoo."

That just pushed them right over the edge. They laughed and laughed, thinking there was no way I was going to do it, but oh yeah, I was going to do it. It wasn't just for me or for my love of Star Wars. It was for spite. To prove that—contrary to what my mother had told me—I was not a pussy. I was going to get that tattoo with a vengeance.

It was around Halloween when we actually got our ink done. Brian and I had planned it all out—go home, meet up with Dan and his then-girlfriend Jaime, and go get our tattoos. Jaime was a bit of a pro at this, or at least she was to us since she had a bunch of them.

"I got a guy," she told us, making it sound like we were asking her to score us meth. "He'll take care of you. No problem."

Jaime was a tiny little thing, so skinny that she didn't get her skin tattooed so much as she had her bones scrimshawed. Leading the way, like a hipster Sacagawea to our fanboy Lewis and Clark, she took us to see her "guy."

Any expectations I had for the tattoo parlor were immediately debunked when I walked in the front door. I had pictured some rat hole, biker-bar-looking dump where a thick fog of smoke and the sounds of George Thorogood would hit us in the face like a hot, sweaty fist the instant walked through the door. Sadly this wasn't the case. It was less biker bar cliché and more badass doctor's office, all fluorescent light and disinfectant white. The walls were decorated with posters of dragons and other fantasy pinups, and the glass cases that filled the waiting room were packed with studs, hoops, and gauges, all ready to be stapled into someone's face, nipple, spine, or vulva. After a minute of poking around, Jamie led us into the back to meet her guy, a round, multicolored dude named Bill who listened to post-grunge fallout, nu metal bands like Disturbed and Staind and had a tattoo of Vegeta from the anime series *Dragon Ball Z* on his forearm. Not surprisingly, the *DBZ* tattoo filled me with a sense of security in light of the badges of geekdom Brian and I were about to have permanently drawn into our flesh.

"Who's first?" Bill asked. With the shakes kicking in, I graciously gave the honors to Brian. He stepped up to the plate and presented Bill with a printout of the design he wanted—the insignia of the Galactic Empire.

The machine Bill used sounded like a big, robotic bee, buzzing around the room at a constant speed in a big, constant circle. The sound never wavered, stopping only for Bill to refill it or wipe away at the blood and ink that had started to accumulate on Brian's calf. Hearing its constant droning was unnerving. I started to get a cold sweat. Maybe Mom and Dad were right. Maybe I couldn't do this.

After about forty-five minutes, Bill took one last swipe with a paper towel, leaned back, and put his machine down.

"Okay," he said to Brian, "take a look."

Brian hopped off the chair, went over to the mirror to inspect it, and gave his seal of approval. Bill put a bandage over the tattoo and ran down the instructions for taking care of it, then stepped out for a smoke.

"Ready, buddy?" Dan asked.

"Not at all, actually."

"It's not that bad," Brian told me as he peeled back a corner of his bandage to inspect his bloody tattoo. "You get used to it pretty quick."

When Bill came back in he sat down, got his gear ready, and told me to take a seat.

"Come on," he said as he patted the bench with a gloved hand. "Hop on up, boyo." Maybe in another life he had been a pediatrician.

As I handed him my printout of the Rebel Alliance's emblem, I shook like something that shakes a lot. I don't know, let's say I was shaking like a leaf or a booty. Deep breaths, deep, soothing breaths were nowhere on the menu. My breathing was erratic and I was quickly making myself lightheaded. Or maybe that was the searing pain in my bicep as Bill sliced into me with what felt like a red hot, serrated knife. I clenched my fists white-knuckle tight.

I tried not to look. It felt like he was tracing the design with a lightsaber. Mom was right. I was a huge pussy. The room started to spin. My head felt like a balloon that someone was filling with hydrogen. All I needed was the slightest spark for my head to blossom into a pathetic flower of flame and gore. It took everything I had to keep my arm still. Finally Bill was done. With the outline.

"How you doin'?" he asked.

"Good," I wheezed. "A little lightheaded."

"Whoa-kay! Tell you what. I'm gonna go have a cigarette. But you? You're gonna sit there and not move too much while your buddies go get you a soda and a candy bar. Sound good?"

I nodded. If I was embarrassed, no one would have been able to tell because blushing just brought the normal color back to my cheeks.

Dan and Brian looked into my face and tried to mask their amusement with forced concern.

"Man, you okay? You want us to get you something?" Dan asked.

"Yeah. Dr. Pepper and some peanut butter cups."

I was such a goon. And such a pussy.

As I washed down the last chocolaty, peanut buttery morsel with a swig of Dr. Pepper, Bill came back. Seeing that I was in better shape, he went back to work. The worst was over. For some reason the filling in of a solid black patch on my arm was infinitely less painful than just the outline.

Finally it was done. Like a woman's name written in big swirly letters on a banner wrapped with barbed wire around a bleeding heart being eaten by a snake crawling out of a skull, I had my very own love letter scribbled on my arm, letting the world know beyond any shadow of a doubt just how big a dork I was for Star Wars.

Sophomore year, as it turned out, was full of small steps and giant leaps. Between semesters that year I had struck up an oddly flirtatious relationship with a girl named Alli. I say oddly because I had just come out of a relationship that was frighteningly similar to the one I'd had with Liz in most respects: emotionally crippling, creatively suffocating, and ever so sexually frustrating. Women, I told myself, were the last things I wanted to be thinking about. Yet there I was, flirting away with a cute freshman on Instant Messenger. Oh yeah, that's another reason why it was odd. It was *all* done through Instant Messenger. Somewhere in those emotionless block letters, between the chirping chimes of a new-message alert, were winks, blushed smiles, and some innocent touching of the arms and shoulders. I didn't give it a whole lot of thought before going back to school for the spring semester. It was just a fun way to pass time when I was up late with nothing to do at my parents' house. But once I was back at school, real things started happen almost immediately.

We were among the first wave of students back on campus after the break, and a snowstorm was rushing our way. Alli and I had been talking—er, typing—when she decided that she was going to spend the duration of the night's storm watching a movie.

"But I don't know what to watch," she typed. "Any suggestions?"

"Well, I planned on watching *The Big Lebowski* myself."

"Oh yeah? I never saw that one."

I invited her over to correct immediately what I saw as a serious problem.

"This isn't an option," I told her. "So unless you decide to reveal that you've never seen *Star Wars*, you're coming over to watch this with me."

We watched the movie in anti-silence. Neither of us spoke a word, but the room roared with the sounds of feelings and urges deep within me, all trying to manifest themselves in the form of a "move." As she sat there, on my bed, my underfed libido kept jabbing me in the ribs with an angry elbow.

She's on your bed! it was telling me. *She's on your fucking bed! Good God, man, do you need a map?!*

When the movie ended I walked Alli to the door. We stood there for a bizarre, hour-long moment while she tried to broadcast a signal on a frequency that my brain wasn't tuned to pick up. There she was, her face framed by an adorable bob, shooting me the green light with her big, brown eyes. I jammed my hands in my pockets to hide the boner that was ready to wage an all-out war against my brain for refusing to acknowledge what was happening.

So help me, Brain, with God as my witness, I will have my revenge if you fuck this up!

We're not that guy, Boner, said my brain. *This doesn't happen to us.* When the tension had hit its peak, Alli finally broke the silence. "Thanks for the movie."

"Yeah. Anytime. I'll see you around."

I shut the door. It wasn't until five minutes later that my brain finally caught wise to what my junk had known all along. *That was a moment, wasn't it?* asked my brain. *One of those Hollywood moments where we're supposed to grab the girl and kiss her.*

There's still time, Brain! You can still make this up to us!

I hopped on my computer and waited, hoping that she'd sign onto Instant Messenger. When she did, I typed fast.

"Thanks for hanging out with me." Enter.

Alli typed back, "No—thank you."

"Do you want to play in the snow with me?" Enter.

Alli typed, "Okay."

"Cool. I'll meet you outside in five." Enter.

I was terrified but ready to dash out the door when familiar theme music started playing on the TV. An episode of *The Venture Bros.* had just started. Alli, I noticed, was still online. Maybe if I asked she'd wait a half-hour. . . .

I couldn't believe it. I knew, or at the very least had a damn good idea, what was going to happen that night. We were probably going to make out long and hard. There might even be a slim chance that I'd get laid. Laid! Here I was, a virgin with a Star Wars tattoo, and I was actually considering asking her to wait until my cartoons were over before I let her take that burdensome virginity off my hands. Torn between the potential promise of sex and getting my geek fix, I sat there wasting precious seconds. Quickly I tried to message her again. If she didn't respond, I'd make *The Venture Bros.* wait. If she did, I'd make her wait. My justification to myself for all of this was that I needed the half-hour to mentally prepare myself. Bullshit. I was just being a total chickenshit about the whole situation—also, I really liked cartoons.

"Hey, you still there?" I asked.

Alli typed, "Yup."

"Cool. Hey, you think you could give me like, half an hour?"

Alli responded, "Sure."

"Thanks," I said, and then in the spirit of full disclosure I added, "a really cool cartoon just started, so I'll be out when it's over."

Here's where I expected her to tell me not to bother. "Cartoons, huh? Nah, I'm gonna go find a Hacky Sack circle or a beer pong game somewhere and get a real man to take me on a whirlwind tour of carnal heights, the likes of which I had never before imagined." Instead she said, "Oh, cool. Well, have fun.

I'll meet you outside in a bit." That was it, no more excuses. I wouldn't let anything else get in my way. I didn't care if George Lucas himself showed up at my dorm room door with an advanced copy of *Revenge of the Sith* on DVD that I had to watch right there at that very moment. There was no way I was going to blow this. Actually, that probably would have been enough for me to risk blowing it, but at this point I think that goes without saying.

After Doc Venture's yard sale was crashed by a bunch of pathetic, bickering supervillains, I threw on a coat and headed out of my dorm into the snow. *Was the window for romance with Alli still open? Was there even a window to begin with? What if I made up 'the moment'?* As these what-ifs ran through my head, I stepped out into what had, over the last couple of hours, become a full-tilt blizzard.

I walked out into the center of the quad and waited for her. When I saw her making her way through the snow, I bent down and armed myself with a snowball. I waited until she waved and smiled, until I saw the whites of her eyes, and then I whipped it at her as hard as I could. My frozen projectile, forged of fear and pent-up lust, hit her square in the face.

"What the fuck!" she squealed before arming herself and fighting back. We hurled snowballs at one another until I could get close enough to grab her by the shoulders and push her into a snow bank. As she fell she hooked her legs around the backs of mine and pulled me down next to her. I lay there on my back laughing and trying to catch my breath, when she rolled on top of me and jammed her tongue into my mouth. Clearly the window was still wide open.

When she pulled her lips away from mine, she looked down at me curiously, her brain processing the hundreds of thousands of calculations per nanosecond to figure out whether or not she'd acted out both of our desires or hers alone.

"Well, hi," I said, cracking my voice for maximum cuteness and comedic effect.

She laughed and kissed me again. I held her tight, her body feeling like an adorable little space heater against my belly while my back was freezing against the snow.

"You want to go in and get warmed up?" she asked. "I can make you some tea."

"I don't like tea." *I don't like tea?* There was a good chance I was going to get laid; who the hell did I think I was to be so picky?

"Hot cocoa?"

"That works."

She smiled and climbed off me, and we walked into her dorm and into her room, where neither tea nor cocoa would ever make an appearance.

Inside we peeled off our wet layers of jackets, gloves, and boots and tossed them into a pile in the corner. It wasn't long before the rest of our clothes joined them and we were throwing ourselves at one another like giant, hairless rabbits while Radiohead and the Smashing Pumpkins played in the background. Halfway through *Adore* she told me there was a condom in her purse if I wanted to go get it.

"I have a confession to make," I said, manning up to bite the bullet. "I've never done this before."

She laughed and said, "Yeah, I can tell." She kissed me hard before rolling off the bed and rummaging through her purse.

When I left Alli's room the next morning, I stepped out into more of the same shitty weather from the night before, but it might as well have been a beautiful, blindingly sunny day with cartoon birds fluttering and chirping around me as I walked back to my dorm. In fact, if I had known the words to "Singin' in the Rain," I probably would have busted them out, hopping up on top of picnic tables, swinging around light poles, and dancing through a foot of snow. Instead, I slowly stomped back to my room through the crunchy accumulation, whistling the TIE fighter attack music from *A New Hope*.

I was impressed with myself. I had experienced those moments a couple of times before, the ones when you have to just lean over and kiss the girl, but I had never hit the ball out of the park. Even the time when I'd managed to get damn near close to going all the way with a girl, it was after weeks of giggling, holding hands, and slowly, quietly making our way around the bases after any parents and siblings had gone to bed. Though I just had that gut feeling about what asking Alli to play in the snow would lead to, I never, in all honesty, really thought I had it in me. A five-year reign of sexual frustration— where at best I'd luck out with the bittersweet release of a hand job, but more often than not wound up with a chaffing wiener thanks to the never-not-humiliating, fully clothed dry hump— had finally come to an end.

"Look, I really, really like you" is probably one of the worst intros for a breakup, because it pretty much says it all right off the bat. There's nowhere good for a sentence to go that starts with "look" and has two "really's" in it. It's a sentence that almost always slides gracefully into a weak-ass, "But I just don't think that I'm in the right place to get into another relationship right now," and when I started saying it to Alli it was no exception.

Alli and I dated for a month or so before I ended things. We had a great time playing together, but I still had all sorts of issues about trust after my last relationship, an excuse that made perfect sense in my head at the time but sounded like a crock of shit when given as the reason for a breakup. It sounds like a stock excuse.

I guess the reason why it all sounded so crappy was because I was leaving out a big reason why I was hesitant to be her boyfriend. Alli was only a freshman, and she was very intense about all the new freedoms and skewed sense of maturity that came with being a college student. What struck her as being very adult struck me as being very annoying, and after only a month I could barely stand to listen to her talk. How do you tell someone that?

"Well, do you still want to be friends?" she asked.

"Yeah, totally. I just don't think that I'd be a very good boyfriend at the moment." This was completely genuine, even if only partially explained.

"Well, I guess I appreciate your being honest with me. It's just too bad."

"Sorry."

"It's okay." Her calm, if disappointed, face started to crack, hinting at a hurt girl who didn't want to reveal herself. "Well, I have some things to do, so, you know. . . ."

"Yeah."

She gave me a hug at her door. I wanted to thank her, but I didn't think that that particular moment was the right time for a "Thanks for making me a man" speech. Instead I gave her an honest "see you around" and walked home.

Back in my dorm I sat alone and aimlessly surfed around the Internet while I reflected on things with Alli. After a few minutes I came across a link for the newest *Revenge of the Sith* trailer. My gears instantly shifted. The final countdown had begun.

CHAPTER 16

NEW LOVE AND LOOMING *REVENGE*

BRIAN AND I HAD NEVER been very good at keeping our opinions to ourselves, and we thought so highly of our tastes that we usually considered our opinions to be fact. Everyone knew us as vehement haters of *Episode I* and *II*, and our response to the long-awaited DVD release of the original trilogy—complete with even more computer-generated additions, including replacing the old ghost of Anakin Skywalker with Hayden Christensen's smarmy mug—was "Thanks for the sweet bonus disc, George, but please, stop fiddling around with our childhood." So when we showed up on campus with our tattoos, we were immediately put under that burning, blinding interrogation light. Our accusers asked, "Why a Star Wars tattoo? Don't you hate the new ones? It's fake, right?"

Yes, we'd tell everyone, we hate the new ones, but the tattoos had nothing to do with those new movies. That explanation would usually be enough to stop the questions, but the eyes kept rolling. And for me there was always an unspoken part of any sentence that started, "Yeah, I hate the new Star Wars movies." The rest of it went, "but the way I see it, he's still got one more chance and he's really cornered himself into telling the parts of the story we've all been waiting for." I kept that second half to myself. On the surface I saw my own optimism as weak and pathetic, but deep down I desperately clung to the belief that *Episode III* would deliver in the end.

That hope was buried deep under five years of disappointment and experience; I knew better than to get too excited. Whenever the topic came up with Brian, I'd confess to really be looking forward to *Revenge of the Sith.*

"Dude, don't do it to yourself," he'd say. "You know you're just setting yourself up to be let down."

"Did you see that new trailer the other night? I sat through an episode of *The O.C.* for that shit, man, and it was fucking worth it!"

The other carrot being dangled in front of me was *The Clone Wars* animated shorts by Genndy Tartakovsky. Stylistically similar to his other series, *Samurai Jack*, the cartoon was a shot in the arm, curing all my Star Wars–related woes. Over the course of thirty short episodes, each ranging from three to twelve minutes, Tartakovsky tapped into the essence of Star Wars better than Lucas had the last two times around. The big battles meant something, and he even managed to give that lame-o Dooku a bit of a purpose. But what really got me was showing Anakin as the ace pilot with a devil-may-care attitude and a chip on his shoulder that would make Beggar's Canyon look like a pothole. It showed a young man with so much promise, natural ability, and fear walking a nail-bitingly thin line. On one side was solid ground, a woman who loved him, and a galaxy at peace thanks to his valor. On the other was a bottomless hole of death, suffering, and a galaxy cowering at his very name.

The issue with all of this is that we know what happens to Anakin Skywalker. We know that he falls to the dark side. That's how we met him. He had already fallen. We know that in the end he manages to claw his way out of that pit, and out of love for his son he is able to rediscover the light. I'd be damned though if millions of fans, myself very much included, didn't want to see those firsts steps on a journey toward the Darth Vader we all know and love to hate. That was the point, wasn't it? At least, I told myself after seeing all the trailers, we will see the final steps in the life of Anakin Skywalker and his rebirth as Vader.

Once again my judgment was clouded by what the trailers gave me—all the sound bites I wanted to hear, the things I wanted to see. I was beginning to feel like a battered girlfriend who kept letting the same asshole back in the door every time he showed up with a box of chocolates tucked under his flannel-clad arm and an apology on his bearded lips.

"I fell down some stairs!" I'd tell friends when they saw me with a black eye and a Jar Jar T-shirt on every three years. "All George is guilty of is loving me too much!"

I even went as far as to put my fears and desperate justifications of the previous two movies' glaring crapulance into my college's newspaper. Here is an excerpt for your consideration:

> All grievances with the previous two films aside, let's get to the real question on many a fanboy's mind, that is, will *Episode III* be able to make up for the sins of the past? While many will argue that it won't, one fact remains, and that is that this is the

movie we've been waiting for. As crappy as *Episode I* and *II* are, they were, and please forgive me for saying this, necessary to get the story to the point that we all expected to see covered over the course of three films. What we've been waiting for is where the shit really hits the fan. We wanted to see how and why all the Jedi were killed, the Old Republic crumbled at its very foundation, and how the Skywalker twins were hidden from their father. But above all else, we wanted to see a battle that defines epic: Obi-Wan Kenobi and Anakin Skywalker slugging it out in a lightsaber duel that puts all others to shame. And while we will finally get to see this scene of Star Wars lore finally acted out, it will determine whether or not Lucas is forgiven or officially written off as dead to legions of fans.

As each day passes and May 19 gets closer, I grow more nervous. To get my hopes up is a sure-fire way to leave disappointed. To not get my hopes up feels wrong. So will I be in the theater on that fateful Thursday? You bet, and on the outside I'll be just as excited as I was when I heard that fanfare play back in 1999, but on the inside I will be telling myself, it can't be any worse than you're expecting it to be. Two hours later I'll leave the theater either asking George to forgive me for doubting him, or with a broken heart that no woman could ever claim credit for (yes, these movies mean THAT much to me).

Desperate! I wanted that movie so bad. So bad! On paper it had everything I needed from it. There was nothing to keep it from delivering. All I had to do was wait it out. Just a few weeks—a month, tops. So doesn't it figure that just when I was ready to slip into some Zen-like, meditative stasis before *Sith*'s release, a girl came waltzing into the picture and made everything about my life more chaotic than it needed to be?

Marion was an older woman, having five years on my twenty and was just finishing with her undergraduate degree. I had met her early on during my freshman year when I started writing at the school paper. She was one of the editors that year and was sort of like a mentor to me in the sense that she was very encouraging and frequently asked me to pick up last-minute assignments. The students at the paper made up most of the friends I had that first year, and it was Marion's welcoming presence that kept me there even after she had graduated.

One Friday night Marion and her roommates had a party where the theme was "anything goes but clothes."

"Basically, if you want to get in the door, you have to wear something that you made," she told me. "No real pants."

People were decked out in suits made out of duct tape, newspapers, aluminum foil, and toilet paper. I decided to make photocopies of a pair of jeans and a T-shirt, color them in with crayon, and staple them to some long johns.

"See," I told her when I walked in, "no real pants, just like you said!"

"Oh my God," she said with her big, trademark smile. "That's amazing."

Over the course of the night we laughed at some people's more half-assed efforts at trying to live up to the party's theme, and we talked about the newspaper. Meanwhile, something was happening, and I was just beginning to realize that it had slowly been happening for a couple of weeks. It was never spoken, just implied through a different kind of body language and something in our eyes. It wasn't a doe-eyed kind of stare, but a probing, almost tremor-in-the-Force kind of look. It was a look that asked what the other was thinking. I remembered all the times during those couple of weeks when I would make it a point to be somewhere if I knew she was going to be there. When someone would mention her name, my ears would perk up. She had become, aside from *Episode III*, all I could think about, and what scared the hell out of me was how casually I was handling it.

Many drinks later, I found myself stripped of my paper duds and left with no choice but to strut proudly around the party in thermal underwear.

"You're a class act, Pacitti," my friend Jim told me between slugs of vodka.

"Don't act like you aren't jealous. This look gets me chicks all the time," I said before turning to Marion and shouting across the room, "Hey! Wanna make out?"

"Sure." She sounded about as interested as someone who had just agreed to go to the mall for no particular reason.

"See," I told Jim. "Long johns. Total babe magnet." I looked back at Marion and saw that she had held her eyes on me despite being actively involved in a conversation on the other side of the room. I smiled, rolled my eyes, and went to get another drink.

Once it was technically Saturday and everyone was good and sauced, Marion and I found ourselves alone on the couch, taking up just one cushion.

"You're funny," she told me as our hands locked into one another and her head slid onto my shoulder.

"Yeah, well, looks aren't everything."

"You're also better than that. That's a bad line, and you know it."

I looked down at her and she rolled her eyes up to meet mine. I tried to think of a genuinely funny comeback, but instead I kissed her. And then we were making out. And then I was noticing that long johns are too revealing for a man in that position. We moved on to her room while the party roared and eventually wound down on the other side of the door.

For the first couple of days after our first hookup, there was an awkward tension between us. I tried not to seem awkward, which, without fail, always made me more awkward. But there was no avoiding each other; we had to work on the new issue of the paper. She was there. I was there. We were both there, and neither of us could look each other in the eye or get any work done.

That week's issue was taking longer than most to put together. By the time the sun came up, there was no end to the work in sight, and everyone on the staff was getting hungry. Marion, being the ever-caring person that she was, volunteered to go get coffee and doughnuts.

"I'll come too!" I meant to say it subtly, like it didn't really matter to me—even though it totally did—if I went with her or not, but I ended up blurting it out with the subtlety of a drumroll fart in the middle of a wedding right after everyone's asked if they have any reason why the bride and groom should not be wed.

The car ride was thankfully short to the nearest Dunkin' Donuts, which in any given town in Massachusetts is usually half a stone's throw away. The trip was made in silence, the two of us shooting quick glances at the other, blushing and trying to figure out how to talk about what had happened a few nights before. Maybe one of us would casually start up a casual conversation about what the other had ordered for breakfast and then we could transition, casually, into the issue of our casual sexual episode. Casually.

"So," Marion started after a frumpy woman with trashy fingernails and a gold chain with her name on it went to get my bagel sandwich, "you want to talk about the other night?"

Or maybe she would just throw it out there.

"Yeah, kind of."

"'Cause you've been a little. . . ."

"Weird?"

"Yeah."

"Yeah, sorry. I don't mean to be, I just. . . ."

"I know." She smiled.

"It's just that—"

"Egg and cheese on a bagel!"

I turned, shot the frumpy woman a dirty look, and grabbed my food out of her orange rhinestone-studded talons. Marion and I took a seat with a nice view of the parking lot and hashed it out.

"I really had a good time the other night," she said, smiling shyly up over her coffee.

"Yeah. Me too."

"But I don't want that to change things between us. I care about you a lot, and our friendship is more important than anything else that may have happened."

"Yeah, you know, same here. So," I took a big bite out of my sandwich, and with a mouth full of imitation egg product, asked, "what do we do now?"

It was decided that we'd keep doing what we had just done. Have a really good time. Enjoy one another's company and all the bonuses that now came with it. Neither of us wanted to dive into a relationship with a month or so left in school, but we didn't want to deny ourselves the pleasure we both got out of that night together.

"I mean, I'm going to be graduating in a month," she said.

"Yeah, no totally. I mean, I'd hate to think I was holding you back. I still have two years of this shit. Plus, I'm really not in any place to start something serious right now."

"It's for the best."

"Absolutely."

We were just Marion and Tony, the same as a week before, only now we'd hook up whenever the mood struck. Which it did. A lot. Like, a lot a lot.

In the following few weeks we learned much about one another—not just physically—which was funny, because we'd been friends for nearly two years. But in those short few weeks we poured our hearts out to each other. She told me what it was like growing up amidst divorce and about her bouts with depression. I shared my insecurities and my feeling that no matter how much ground I ever gained, I always sort of felt like the odd man out. We shared our passions, both of us wanting to make something of ourselves as writers. And of course I talked endlessly about Star Wars. For a bit there it seemed as if I had not a care in the world. My paranoia about being betrayed by my beloved movie was pushed for the first time in weeks to the back burner. I pined and I pleaded, I ranted and raved, and she never once rolled her eyes. No girl—friend, girl-friend, or other—had ever not rolled her eyes when I got going on my Star Wars soapbox.

"You know," she said one night while we were lying in her bed, having thoroughly exhausted one another, "when I was a kid I had a couple of pet hamsters named Artoo and Threepio."

"I think that's the hottest thing I've ever heard."

"Shut up and kiss me, nerd!"

We clung to each other while we slowly, and very nakedly, drifted off to sleep.

Marion was the first girl I had ever met who didn't make me feel like I had to put up some sort of front. With Liz and the few girls I had dated between her and Marion, I inhabited an alternate identity. I looked and thought the same way I always had, but certain traits were accented or toned down depending on the girl, and I never noticed it until the relationship started winding down. I felt like a radio, ever so slightly out of tune. There was static over who I really was, who I knew I wanted to be, but I could still hear that person enough to settle for listening through the crackle and white noise.

With Marion I didn't need to settle. With Marion there was no static, just a crystal-clear satellite feed. We were both coming through to each other in high-definition digital clarity. The only problem was the knowledge that I was starting to feel for her in ways that weren't stated in the definition of our pseudo-relationship. I had to keep that in check. Somehow I had to keep those feelings at bay.

CHAPTER 17

DON'T SITH IN MY MOUTH AND CALL IT A SUNDAE

THE LAST NIGHT I STAYED with Marion was the night before a final exam. I was so unprepared for it that I thought I might get a better grade by not showing up at all. Still, at quarter of eight that morning I dragged myself out of Marion's arms, rummaged around for my underpants, and scrambled to wing my way through that final.

"Good luck," she said as I fumbled to yank my pants on over my shoes, which I had managed to locate first.

"In my experience there's no such thing as luck," I told her. Seeing her confused look, I added, "Obi-Wan said it."

I kissed her and somehow made it to class on time. My body was running on the fumes of cheap vodka and the thrill of having stayed up until five, rolling around with a naked girl in a small, university-issued bed-for-one. Everything ached in the best sort of way.

The exam was for Studies in Multimedia, a class where the idea was to learn the subliminal language of art. Film, paintings, advertising, and literature—they all contain clues in the obvious that suggest something greater beneath the surface. I was fascinated up until the point where my professor started talking during the very first class that semester. He had such a stiff, lifeless voice that you couldn't help but feel like balling up your sweatshirt and putting your head down for a quick little coma. He was old, or so I was told. His body seemed to suggest that he was only in his late fifties, but his voice pegged him more in the vicinity of near-death. He wouldn't get a response out of that class if he'd had a smoking gun in his hand and a pile of executed bodies behind him.

"The exam has three questions," he explained, his voice sounding like a cross between a creaky old rocking chair and anesthesia. "I expect you to spend at least forty-five minutes on each one. Any less than that and you won't have answered it thoroughly enough for my liking."

As our professor walked around the class I couldn't help but revisit the previous night's, and current morning's, goings on. I was madly in love with Marion and I half expected my exam to be riddled with sweet nothings and romantic musings about the girl of my dreams. Either that or the physical strain of writing my name would be enough for me to black out from exhaustion. Finally the professor handed me my blue book. I cracked open a pen and put my shoulder into it. Thirty-seven minutes later I handed him my completed exam. I made it back to my dorm, lay down, and slept through two meals.

Later that night was the last time Marion and I saw each other as whatever it was the two of us had become. We took a walk around the campus through a fog so thick that it looked and felt like there was nothing in the world except us, the ground we stood on, and some fuzzy balls of light shining from somewhere deep in the mist. We parked ourselves in the campus amphitheater, already full of chairs for the graduation ceremony that was now just a week away.

"When are you heading out?" she asked.

"Early. Right after my last final, so noon, probably."

She took a deep breath as she thought about how she was going to say what was clearly ready to jump off the tip of her tongue.

"I know that we said we were just going to enjoy the time we had with one another and sort of leave it at that, but I really . . . ." She took another deep breath. I tried not to look at her. "I really think that you're someone I could see myself with."

I felt her look away from me and down to her rattling knees. Mine were shaking too. I was torn. I wanted Marion desperately and I believed her when she said she wanted to be with me too, but I honestly had no idea how long it could all last. Her real, adult life was about to start, whereas I still had two years of school, two years of riding with my grown-up training wheels. How often would I see her? How long would it be until the bottom fell out and things just came crumbling down? Was it worth it to commit myself to such an unknown, especially one that was probably looming a lot closer than either of us wanted to admit?

I couldn't help but feel that there'd be a fair amount of heartache no matter what I chose, and in spite of how I knew I felt about her, I decided to get all of the sad shit out of the way sooner rather than later. My justification for all of it was that, if nothing else, at least we could say we had ended it on the best note possible.

"Look, Marion, I don't know if I can do it. You're graduating. Neither of us knows where you'll be after that. I just don't want to be in a position where I'm afraid that I'll be holding you back." I sounded about as whiny as Luke did when he told Obi-Wan that he couldn't go with him to Alderaan, and just like Luke, I hid behind a veil of untruths, because what it all boiled down to was that I was afraid of the big unknown tomorrow that came with saying "I think so too."

Her chin sank down to her chest as a big, crushed tear ran down the cheek closest to me.

"I understand," she said.

We leaned into each other, forehead to forehead, while we whispered sweet things about how much we meant to each other and how happy we were to have at least had that time together. We kissed one last time and sat holding each other and crying just a little.

When we finally got up, Marion took my hand.

"Do you want to come back and stay the night?" she asked me.

"No," I said, wondering if and when I might ever regret that decision. "No, I think I should just head back." I regretted it instantly.

After rushing through whatever my last exam was the next morning, I checked out of my dorm, jumped into my car, and headed home. The events that had transpired the night before, and to a much greater extent the ones that didn't, haunted me. My dreams were a montage of futures that could have been and my internal monologue had become condescending for letting such a sure thing slip away. With a foot to the floor I made it home in record time, hopped on the computer, and sent Marion the following:

marion,

okay...here's the deal. i hate myself right now. i hate myself because i feel like i made a huuuuuuuuge mistake. i hate myself because i feel like telling you that i'm not ready for a relationship, that i'm afraid to get hurt is a cop out. i hate myself because you marion are something else, something amazing and i've never met someone like you. i hate myself because i think i may have blown the chance of ever finding out what being your boyfriend is like. i hate myself for not going back with you monday night.

i know this is probably the last thing you wanted to hear or read because as if this all weren't confusing enough i throw this into the mix. i'm just tired of living a life of what if? i want this particular "what if?" answered. what if you and me decided to pursue something with one another? i've been hating myself and the only thing that has been on my mind is you. think about it. I'll understand either way and still be your friend always, so dont worry about hurting my feelings or anything. i just needed to say it. I should have said it the other night but i just got too afraid and couldnt make the words come out...well here they are now... do with them what you feel is right.

—tony

I waited impatiently, checking my e-mail every ten minutes. I finally heard back later that night. The e-mail has since been lost, but it went something to the effect of "It wouldn't work. I'm not in the right place in my life for this, but we'll always have our friendship and that short time together."

I don't remember what I said in response. It could have been anything, though e-mail records—which as luck would have it, only saved the mail I sent and none that I received—indicate that I responded with absolutely nothing. I was speechless, heartbroken, and exhausted. In hindsight, the breakup was for the best. That quick jab to the heart always feels better than a slow stab and a few twists, which is probably what would have happened if we'd dated and it all came crashing down. But who's to say it would have come crashing down? I didn't know that for a fact, but I told myself that it would have so I'd feel like I had avoided the greater pain. It was a miserable way to kick off the summer, especially with *Revenge of the Sith* opening that week.

On opening day, and with about an hour left before the movie started, I knocked on Brian's parents' door, knowing full well that he wasn't home for the summer yet. His mom answered the door and I asked in a bright, little-kid voice, "Can Tommy come out and play?"

With Tommy, Brian's twelve-year-old brother, in the car, I put it to the floor and bombed down to the same theater where I had seen each of the previous Star Wars prequels. I left a message for Brian's mom to deliver to him: "Tony has Tommy and your ticket; call him when you get to the mall." On the way I unloaded my fears for the movie on Tommy, though most of what I dumped on him were actually thinly veiled regrets about what had happened with Marion.

"Sometimes you go see a movie because the previews are just phenomenal—I mean, they absolutely blow you away. And when you get there and the movie starts, you're totally sold, man. You just love every minute of it. Until the end. You don't want it to end and it almost seems like the director doesn't either, but both of you know that it has to. But who says it has to? There are long movies, tons of them! But it ends all the same and suddenly you're checking your e-mail every three minutes and not sleeping for days and all you want to do is just go back and tell her, 'Yes! I think we should try this!' You know what I mean, Tommy?"

"Uh ... not really?"

Tommy was fortunate to be young enough to enjoy movies uninhibited by the burdens of knowing any better. Part of me envied him, was jealous of his being just at that right age where anything that looked cool and fun and exciting—even if it was as forced as I thought some of the stuff from the new movies was—was enough to make him happy.

Anxiety began to take hold of me as we sat in the movie theater waiting for Brian.

"Where the fuck—sorry—where the heck is he?"

"It's okay," Tommy said. "I know that word."

When my nerves were at their peak, when I thought for sure that I was going to have to go through this ordeal alone, Tommy pointed and waved.

"There he is. See, he wasn't going to miss it."

Brian arrived just in time for the previews, and the three of us sat, waiting either for salvation or for the final blow to be dealt. I still clung to hope. It was all I had in the wake of the emotional tilt-a-whirl I had just taken a ride on with Marion. All I wanted was for this to live up to my expectations. If the girl of my dreams was going to be out of reach,

at least I could have the Star Wars movie I had been waiting
my whole life for.

If the early reviews were to be believed, then the planets
were aligned in my favor. Critics were eating it up this time
around. Some were even saying it was the best in the series
after *The Empire Strikes Back.* Hype ultimately beat me into
submission. "Please, George," I silently pleaded. "Please don't
let me down."

For the last time in my life, the lights went down, the
drumroll started, and "A long time ago in a galaxy far, far away
. . ." came up on the big screen to an eruption of applause and
whistling. The cheers subsided, the text scroll started, and over
the next two hours and some-odd minutes, I learned the true
meaning of heartbreak.

The Clone Wars had been all but skipped over as the
movie threw us into the thick of the wars' last days. Zipping
in and out of lasers, rockets, and other ships were Anakin and
Obi-Wan in what would have been the end all-be all of video
game intros. I was minutes in and the knot in my stomach was
already feeling too tight for my liking. It was not a good way
to start things off.

Images seemed to whiz around the screen at me without
relent. Artoo was suddenly Inspector Gadget and the Three
Stooges all rolled into one, laying oil slicks and booby traps
with handy gizmos he never had in the original trilogy to
thwart a legion of clumsy, goofball robots. The bizarre cyborg
warlord General Grievous limped around the screen coughing
like an asthmatic because coughing explained that he was once

a living, breathing creature better than any sort of actual expo-
sition. Grievous was cool in design, but the explanation for
him never went much deeper than showing that he was kind of
a man and kind of a robot, and he could hold four lightsabers
while making his wrists spin. Like the once-organic character
himself, Grievous had little meat to him.

Eclipsing all of that was another truckload of stiffly delivered melodrama between Anakin and a very pregnant Padmé,
all culminating in her actually saying, "You're breaking my
heart!" with all the feeling you would expect from someone
reading off a cue card in a big, green room. Samuel L. Jackson
went out like a chump at the hands of an overacting Darth
Sidious. Actually all of the Jedi went out like chumps. These
warriors of heightened sense and skill, who were allegedly in
touch with a mystical energy as old as the universe, were systematically shot in the back by a bunch of clones of a guy whose
head had been so easily lopped off by Jackson in *Episode II*.

By the time Anakin had completely succumbed to the dark
side, the movie managed to kick things into high gear with
the final confrontation between Kenobi and Skywalker. It's an
intense scene, a bit grittier than the other lightsaber battles
of the new trilogy, and it was definitely the strongest point of
the movie, but six years and seven-ish hours of crap can't be
justified by twenty minutes of "Okay, I guess that was kind of
neat." Besides, even that brief stretch of cool couldn't sustain
itself to the end of the movie. Never knowing when to leave
well enough alone, Lucas gave us the Darth Vader we all knew,
fully adorned in his jet-black armor and fresh off the operating table. And what did he do when he heard that Padmé was
dead? He yelled "*Noooooo!!!*" like an actor in an Ed Wood film.
Not even some pissed, primordial roar from a man who had

been to hell and back while he ripped the room to pieces with the Force. I half expected a close-up to show tears running down his helmet. Fucking weak.

In the final moments, with the Skywalker twins being shuttled off into hiding, the movie finally took the shape of the one I had seen in my head as a kid growing up wondering "What came before all of this?" The music that played while Luke looked out at Tatooine's binary sunset in *A New Hope* came up as a devastated Obi-Wan Kenobi approached Owen Lars with the infant son of Skywalker. With child in hand, Owen walked past his homestead, watching the same two suns go down.

The music swelled and I felt nothing. The scene was sublime. It was exactly the way—no, the only way—that that movie could have ended. I didn't give a shit. I was fuming. Cue the credit music and the cheering crowd. We're talking standing-ovation kind of noise here. I turned to Brian and Tommy and with no hint of pleasure in my voice dared to be the only one in the audience to ask the question that I felt so desperately needed to be asked.

"What the fuck?!"

I couldn't believe how bad it was. There was no grace period when I thought that it was at least better than the others. It wasn't even that. It was offensive on all levels, even more than the other two. Packed to the gills with fan service—hey look, it's Chewbacca! Remember him? Wink, wink!—sloppy narrative, and its dependence on a "better than the rest of it" last twenty minutes to piggyback the film into our hearts, *Revenge of the Sith* was hands down the worst of the worst in the case of the Star Wars prequels. It was a kick in the balls. It was an April Fool's Day prank that came a month and a half too late and went way over the line.

I thought about all the glowing reviews. Those critics should have been ashamed of themselves! No one should get a pass like that. George Lucas had become his own tragic hero: he gave the world the hope and wonder and joy of the original trilogy as a young devil-may-care filmmaker, only to become obsessed with none of the things that made them so great, and in the end he perverted them into his dark vision. Darth Lucas, Dark Lord of the Sith, made his presence known to me on May 19, 2005. I couldn't help but feel like Obi-Wan, looking upon the burnt and broken husk of Anakin, crying out from a ravaged heart for all the things that his best friend had done and none that he was supposed to—"Bring balance to the Force, not leave it in darkness!" George was supposed to bring the saga full circle, not leave it in ruin!

There were no more certainties in my life. None. In a matter of days I had let the girl of my dreams slip through my fingers and lost my faith in the only thing I ever truly believed in. I never would have thought that a world could exist where I was so angry with Star Wars. It shouldn't have been true; it was impossible, but as sure as Vader is Luke's father, the ugly, painful truth was impossible to ignore.

When I got home my family was waiting eagerly for the verdict. I stepped through the door and my mother, father, and sister all leaned on the edge of the couch, looking at me with ever-questioning eyes, trying to gauge my feelings from my expression and body language. At last Mom broke the silence.

"So?" she asked, her voice unable to contain her excitement. She too had been hooked by the hype. "How was it?"

I lifted my heavy eyes to meet hers. My broken heart counted a couple of beats while her face changed from anticipation to sad commiseration.

"I don't want to talk about it."

I didn't want to talk about anything. Without another word, I went upstairs. My mom, dad, and sister watched as I trudged to my room. It was just after seven in the evening, the sun was still up, and I went to bed. Hating myself. Hating Marion.

Hating Star Wars.

CHAPTER 18

WE'LL ALWAYS HAVE CLOUD CITY

A CHARLIE BROWN KIND OF rain cloud hung over my head for some time in the wake of the saga's coming full circle. They say that time heals all wounds and yes, with Marion, time eventually did, but when you've fallen madly, head over heels in love with someone, you never think you'll ever get over it. Consoling sentiments like "There's plenty of other fish in the sea" are more of a reminder of your failure and lack of any sort of luck in the realm of love. Whether they know it or not, when your friends say something like that to you they are actually rubbing your nose in your own misery.

But sometimes you'll surprise yourself. Sometimes you'll bump into the one that got away at a party a year or so down the road and not feel weird about it. Marion and I had one of these run-ins at a friend's birthday party. It was the first time in several encounters since we'd parted ways where we were able to have a normal, awkward pause–less conversation. Even better was that, in a momentary lapse of judgment, I ended up sleeping with the birthday girl. It might not have been the best idea, but as far as first steps on the road to recovery go, it's not the worst thing I could have done. Clearly I was over Marion, at least over her enough to embark on a series of intermittent flings, good times, and dead-end relationships. The idea of loving someone, however, was still nowhere on the menu. Missing out on all the joy that comes with the *L* word was a sacrifice I was willing to accept if it meant protecting myself from the equally powerful pain that usually came with it. It would be a while before I let a girl get closer to me than several arm's lengths, but I was taking the steps in the right direction. Well, it was some direction.

But not all heartbreaks smooth over so, er, smoothly. More often than not you keep bumping into the person, again and again, and it's not okay. At all. You go to do things that used to make you happy, but now they stink of that heartbreaking bitch. You try to put it out of your head, but you can't. Every time you look in the mirror you're reminded of that person because you have her name tattooed to your arm. You long for the good old days, when you two were happy, but they're gone, and half the time you can't even remember those oh-so-fond memories of what once was. *Fuck you, Time. I thought we were friends! You said you'd make me feel better!*

Star Wars fell into that latter category of gaping, mortal wounds being operated on by that shaky-handed med school dropout called Time. I couldn't stomach what Star Wars had become, and to make matters worse, I couldn't even go back to the old ones to remember what I had loved so much about them. I tried, but the damage was done. Watching my favorite movies just made me bitter. So I didn't watch them. Not for a long, long time.

This sinking feeling even went beyond Star Wars. Movies in general were no longer magic portals to adventure and excitement. My expectations never built up to much more than casual interest. The only real feelings I had as a big movie came rolling down the pike were fear that it would fail to live up to its potential and disdain for the ruining of another great idea or franchise. Even when I'd see a good movie, a movie that I didn't have to dig through desperately to find any redeeming qualities, I was suddenly more critical than ever. I questioned every frame, overthought even the stuff that was meant to be pure entertainment fluff. Nothing was good enough anymore. A lot of the time I'd leave the theater feeling nothing. Friends would be raving and I'd be ambivalent at best.

"What'd you think?" they'd ask. "Wasn't that great?"

I'd shrug. "Yeah, I guess that was okay. I guess."

"Okay? We just watched what has been called the greatest film of all time! Orson Welles's zombie corpse came back from the dead just so he could write a letter to *Variety* saying as much, and all you can say is 'it was okay'?"

It was like asking someone who had lost his sense of taste if something tasted good. Thanksgiving dinner. A Big Mac. An ice-cream sundae. Yeah, of course these are all good; they're delicious things. Everyone knows it, but quite frankly I just didn't give a shit because it didn't matter to me anymore.

When *Revenge of the Sith* came out on DVD, it became a hot-button issue. Friends of mine knew where I stood on the movie—in the minority.

"Hey, know what comes out on Tuesday?" my friend Connor asked one Friday night.

"Fuck you," I answered, knowing that he was just trying to get a rise out of me. Behind us in the parking lot of our dorms, a group of people were circled around two dudes duking it out with those really fancy lightsaber replicas that the theater ushers had carried on the day *Attack of the Clones* opened.

"No, seriously, know what comes out?"

"Fuck you for liking it!"

"Snob."

Wherever I went, I was the guy who didn't like *Revenge of the Sith*, something no one understood and something that frequently resulted in my being accused of not loving Star Wars enough. As time went on and more movies came and went, I was promoted from being "The Guy Who Hated *Episode III*" to "The Guy Who Hated Everything." I'd argue that my tastes were refined, that while I still wanted the sci-fi thrills and comic-book chills that made me love movies as a kid, I also wanted some depth with it. I wanted something real. Instead I got cash-ins and the easy movies that studios knew fanboys would love because they had to (I'm looking at you, *Spider-Man 3*). In reality I was just a bitter, scorned ex-lover of Star Wars in particular and the cinematic experience in general.

By my last semester at college, *Revenge of the Sith* was two years behind me and I had finally gotten myself to a place where I felt I could try to watch Star Wars again. Not just the good ones either, but all of them. Thanks to free HBO at school, I was treated to a marathon of epic proportions. Six movies. One saga. All in a row. It was going to be my chance to really see the new ones for the travesties they were, side by side with the things my childhood fantasies were made of.

That night I had a hearty dinner of a Double Quarter Pounder with Cheese, a medium order of fries, and a ten-piece Chicken McNugget. After a quick stop at the liquor store for

some PBR, whiskey, and some snacks from the mini-mart, I
was set to go. I settled into the couch, knowing full well that
once I started, I was only getting up to replenish my booze,
take a leak, or, in the end, go to bed. Never at any point was
eye contact with the screen to be broken, and silence was to
be maintained at all times. When my roommates and some
friends from down the hall came in somewhere during *Phantom Menace*, one of the girls asked for a bottle opener. She
invoked a fanboy possessed.

"How about I just smash the neck off the bottle on the
counter for you, and you try not to cut your lips up or swallow any glass as you drink it?!" I snarled, unable to control the
venom that spewed from my mouth at an innocent bystander
who neither understood nor appreciated the absurd importance of the ritual I was going through.

Out of the first half of the marathon, the final two-ish hours
were the hardest, but I got through them. Up until that point I
had only seen *Revenge of the Sith* once, the day it opened. Brian,
our roommate Ricky, and I giggled our way through *Sith*, with
Vader's "*Noooooo!!!*" pushing us close to pants-wetting territory.
It was all very cathartic, like telling an embarrassing private
story about an ex that she'd just as soon take to her grave than
share.

"Oh God," I sighed, "it feels good to laugh again."

When *A New Hope* started rolling, I was expecting to be
taken back to a happier time, when I was young and innocent
and didn't overthink movies quite so much. That didn't happen
exactly. Greedo's shooting first still made me twitch. Adding
dialogue to the Emperor's teleconference with Vader in *Empire*
still made me grit my teeth. Hayden's ghost at the end of *Jedi*
still made me pull my hair out. Yes, watching all six made the
new trilogy's inferiority stand out that much more, but it also

reconfirmed just how far the original trilogy had changed from the movies I knew as a kid. As semi-depressing as it was to revisit the whole saga like that, I found myself taking my first steps toward reaching a point of calm about the whole ordeal.

Star Wars wasn't mine. It wasn't anybody but George Lucas's, in terms of the actual, physical movies. He could do whatever he wanted to them because they were his to do them with.

One summer when I was a kid I had a space opera of my own going. I made the ships and bases with LEGOs, and the characters mirrored Luke, Han, and Vader. But as I got new LEGOs to build new ships or introduce new characters, parts of the ongoing story would change, be rewritten, or get ignored altogether. It was still the same story, but I was ultimately in control to change it when new and better LEGO kits became available to me. In the end it all made me happy and satisfied my creative urges. I mean, it was hard not to tweak the history of my little epic as cooler toys came along. George did the same thing. As his toys got more high-tech, he was able to change his story to better fit the one he had supposedly always seen in his head.

Physically, legally, creatively—those are the ways in which Star Wars belong to George Lucas. The only part of them that is mine is the emotional attachment. The memory of sitting on the couch on a sunny day in July watching *The Empire Strikes Back* instead of going outside to get ragged on. The wide-eyed lust for dogfights over the Death Star, the devilish smirk I'd mimic when Han Solo flashed his. The devastation of learning that Vader was Luke's father, and the joy at good winning out over evil when he redeemed himself and killed the Emperor. All the jump-starts to the imagination those movies gave me as a kid, and still give me in my adult life. Above all else, the comfort and security they gave me when I was a scared little kid, and the friendships they served as the mutual basis for. Star Wars had been there for me during those toughest formative years when I really needed it.

By the time *Phantom Menace* came out, I needed to start to face the world on my own, to pick myself up off the ground, and it was time for Star Wars to serve as some other kid's security blanket. I finally believed, honestly and truly believed, that no matter what George had done or would do to Star Wars, nothing could ever really change that. Star Wars and I had become like Ingrid Bergman and Humphrey Bogart in *Casablanca*. They'll always have Paris. We'll always have that HBO bootleg of *Empire*.

EPILOGUE

A MONTH OR SO AFTER seeing *The Clone Wars* with Marc and his mom, I got wind that an outdoor screening of *Star Wars* was happening downtown. The question of whether or not I should attend never crossed my mind. It was a requirement on an intrinsic, primal-instinct level.

Now, it isn't every day that you see a Jedi Knight walking the streets of Providence, Rhode Island. The city isn't home to any sci-fi conventions or other big fan-appreciation events, so there's really no reason for people to walk around dressed up like Obi-Wan Kenobi or an Imperial scout trooper unless it's just something that they like to do. But if anything is capable of bringing the Wookiees out of the woodwork, it's an outdoor screening of *Star Wars*. As I locked up my bike and made my way toward the screen downtown, I saw them: a group of fully decked-out Jedi Knights, strutting their way toward the crowd and ready to entertain the little kids who were visibly excited by their presence.

"You're all here to see *Harry Potter*, right?" one of the middle-aged guardians of galactic peace and justice jokingly asked as he fired up his lightsaber. The kids all laughed and asked if they could try it out or get their pictures taken with him and his accomplices, two other Jedi and a slightly chubbier-than–Harrison Ford Han Solo. I watched from my seat at the corner of the bocce court that served as an outdoor movie theater once a week during the summer months. From down the street I spotted a couple more costumes—a Rebel Alliance soldier and an Imperial Royal Guard—making their way toward the large crowd of people assembled to watch *Star Wars* outside on that beautiful September evening.

"Check this dude out," I overheard a guy next to me saying, pointing at the Royal Guard. "Why the hell would you dress up like that?"

Here, I thought, was the inevitable moment where some dick decides he needs to cut down the people brave enough to appear in public wearing silly costumes. It was the moment that I had feared so much that I never risked appearing in public in a silly costume myself. I waited and listened for the cracks to come, hoping that they'd just get it all out of their system and not ruin the movie by making fun of the fanboys all night.

"Seriously," his friend said, "why not dress up as a stormtrooper or something? All these guys ever did was stand around waiting to get dismissed."

"Leave us!" said the first guy, doing his best impression of Emperor Palpatine ordering the guards out of his chamber. I was pleasantly surprised by his response, which I do agree with. The Royal Guards were pretty useless in the movies, though he neglected to take into account that they did have a cool-enough look to get away with just standing around all day. My paranoia, an old habit that despite my best efforts had chosen to die hard, subsided.

The kids were having a blast as they smiled for their parents' cameras and shot questions at the Jedi quicker than Han shot Greedo.

"Did you make these?" one boy asked, tugging at the man's sleeve.

"Yessir, they're all homemade," he told the kid.

"Why?" another kid asked.

"Because we love Star Wars!" he responded as if it was a silly question to ask. This was followed by wide-eyed "oohs" and "aahs" as the youngsters imagined what household products their parents wouldn't miss while they tried to assemble lightsabers of their own.

When the costumed fans had satisfied the children's relentless curiosity as well as they could, they waved goodbye and walked off to find a good seat. As they passed by me, I approached them with my phone in hand. I had never used my cell phone's camera feature, having always stuck to my stubborn belief that phones should just be phones and that if I needed a camera, I'd have brought one with me. I guess I never banked on meeting an honest-to-goodness Knight of the Old Republic.

"You mind if I get your picture?" I asked.

"Absolutely not. That's what we're here for."

Like a total goon I fiddled with my phone and tried to get the camera function working while two of the Jedi and the Rebel soldier posed, waiting.

"Honestly, I don't even know how to use this damn thing," I confessed like somebody's not-so-tech-savvy dad.

The Rebel soldier tried to help me out, never breaking from his battle-ready stance.

"Is there a menu button? Hit that, then options. There should be a camera button there somewhere."

The man had made the right call in going with a Rebel soldier's uniform. He was too helpful and too polite to have been a stormtrooper. I was sure that if there had been a woman dressed as Princess Leia at the movie that night she would have told him how happy she was to have men like him serving on her ship.

I snapped the picture as the three of them posed there with their homemade blasters and lightsabers. There is nothing particularly awe inspiring about middle-aged men and women in funny robes and leg wrappings holding flashlights with long, green tubes sticking out of the tops of them, but in the picture they look like the real deal. I didn't see a couple of toys being held up by fanatical hobbyists in the photo; I saw two real Jedi Knights wielding blades of righteous light. I could practically hear them humming on my cell phone's screen.

I thanked them for giving me a minute of their time and admitted somewhat falsely to being too lazy to make a costume myself.

"But I do have this," I said as I rolled up my right sleeve, revealing the emblem of the Rebel Alliance tattooed to my bicep.

"All right!" said the Jedi with an enthusiastic thumbs-up. "I'm getting mine in a couple weeks."

I shook the man's hand, told him to enjoy his night, and settled back into my seat on an uncomfortable wooden bench to watch a movie I'd seen countless times and could replay in my sleep. I checked out the crowd. There were plenty of people who were old enough to have seen Star Wars back in '77, but there were also a good chunk of us who hadn't even been born yet. There were even a handful of kids—the ones who had their picture taken with the Jedi—who hadn't been born until two prequels ago.

On the corner of Westminster and Union, which was packed with fans from all walks of life, there was a tangible excitement to the air. It was almost as if the Force itself was actually flowing through us. *Star Wars* is the film that best exemplified the kind of magic movies are capable of. It's the movie whose impact still to this day is sending waves across the ever-growing ocean of our collective cultural consciousness. Why else would parents, more than three decades after the movie's original release, be dragging their kids to an outdoor screening at dusk on a school night to see it?

As the sun finally sank down low enough and that familiar fanfare kicked up, I was overwhelmed by a wave of nostalgia. Suddenly I started to feel like a kid, but not like I felt when I was a kid, a sensation that would have instantly left me socially paralyzed, utterly terrified, and sitting in pants full of my own pee. Instead I felt giddy, free from thoughts of the grown-up world outside our crammed little street corner. In that moment there was nothing more important than the images up on the screen and the fact that all of the strangers sitting around me were my friends for those brief couple of hours that we shared together under George Lucas's stars.

ACKNOWLEDGMENTS

Before anyone else, I need to thank my parents. Dad never questioned the choices I've made and always believed that somehow I'd know how to land on my feet. Mom, on the shittiest Christmas either of us had ever had, told me, "You're dead for a very long time, my friend, and I for one am not going down without a fight and some vodka in my veins." Without their bottomless love, support, and sage-like musings, I wouldn't be whatever it is I am today. Now the rest of you:

The people at Adams Media, particularly Karen Cooper, Paula Munier, Wendy Simard, and Beth Gissinger for their enthusiasm and faith in somebody no one had ever heard of and his first book. Elisabeth Lariviere and Heather M. Padgen for their careful dedication. My editors, Matt Glazer and Jennifer Hornsby, for reigning in my incessant fanboy ramblings.

Craig Seymour for being such a supportive friend and mentor from the earliest days of what would become this book.

Brian, Dan H., and Rich for facilitating video game, booze, and *Magic: the Gathering*-related distractions. Thea for being my Sunday night shrink. Amanda for finding the "Rectum of Doom." Sara and Karen of Mortified Boston for thinking it'd be a good idea to let me read about Hitler's ghost onstage. Sondra for helping me with my Rebel flight suit. Kendall, Allison, and Marlaina for feedback early on. My coworkers at Pastiche Fine Desserts for putting up with my poop jokes, frequent bad days, and sloppy plate designs. Scott and Laura for pointing me in the right direction. And to all the friends who didn't get mentioned: don't think for a moment that our adventures together haven't meant the world to me.

Lastly, I would like to thank George Lucas. His creations have, and always will be, my security blanket.